THE PRINCE OF CENTRE-HALVES
THE LIFE OF TOMMY 'T.G.' JONES

THE PRINCE OF CENTRE-HALVES
THE LIFE OF TOMMY 'T.G.' JONES

Rob Sawyer

First published as a hardback by deCoubertin Books Ltd in 2017.

First Edition

deCoubertin Books, Studio I, Baltic Creative Campus, Liverpool, L1 OAH
www.decoubertin.co.uk

ISBN: 978-1-909245-54-9

Cover design and typeset by Thomas Regan | Milkyone Creative.

Printed and bound by Standart.

In loving memory of Louise Hitchmough (1967–2016)
Greatly missed sister, friend and fellow Evertonian

CONTENTS

AUTHOR'S NOTES

FOR THIS BOOK, I WAS FACED WITH THE DILEMMA OF HOW to refer to Thomas George Jones. While he is best known as 'Tommy' in his homeland, his friends and family often shortened this to 'Tom'. In English football circles, on Merseyside in particular, he was referred to by his initials: 'T.G.' For consistency, I refer to him as 'T.G.' throughout this biography, except when directly quoting articles or interviewees. Those interviewed frequently interchanged 'Tommy', 'Tom' and 'T.G.' – sometimes within the same sentence. In such instances, I have not amended the monikers used.

Transcripts of three interviews with T.G. have provided invaluable source material for this biography. John Rowlands, Rogan Taylor and Andy Smith all spoke with T.G. during the course of researching their respective books: Everton Football Club: 1878–1946, Three Sides of the Mersey, and The Complete Centre Forward: The Authorised Biography of Tommy Lawton. I am grateful to John, Rogan, and Andy, as well as John Williams and Andrew Ward, who generously gave me access to these fascinating interviews.

Either side of the Second World War, the Merseyside sports scene was blessed with a cadre of talented journalists – most of whom used sobriquets. The likes of Ernest Edwards (often writing as Bee) and his son Leslie (who inherited the Bee byline from his father), Don Kendall (Pilot), Joe Wiggall (Stork), Louis T. Kelly (Stud Marks) and Bob Prole (Ranger) delivered in-depth, perceptive and pithy reporting on Everton affairs. I am fortunate that Billy Smith has transcribed so much of their output onto his Blue Correspondent website (www.bluecorrespondent.co.nr).

Where appropriate, I have used the current Welsh spelling of locations. However, where the names of publications were anglicised at the time, I have used those (e.g. Caernarvon and Denbigh Herald, as opposed to Caernarfon and Denbigh Herald). Any errors are entirely my own. I have tried to attribute all sources where possible, but some newspaper cuttings I had access to came with nothing to indicate their provenance. For brevity I have referenced the most commonly quoted sources in superscript as follows:

Andy Smith interview with T.G. – AS
John Rowlands interview with T.G. – JR
Rogan Taylor interview with T.G. – RT
Liverpool Echo – LE
Liverpool Football Echo – FE
Daily Post – DP
Liverpool Evening Express – EE
Caernarvon and Denbigh Herald – CDH
North Wales Chronicle – NWC
Western Mail – WM
Everton match-day programme – EP
Everton board of directors minutes – BM
Harlech Television/HTV – HTV

FOREWORD

Dr David France

MY EARLY CHILDHOOD WAS COLOURED BY THE DEAN VERSUS Lawton debate. Bill 'Dixie' Dean was the champion of my grandfather, Tommy Lawton the hero of my father. They were united, however, in their opinion of who was the finest centre-half in the land: that was the unflappable T.G. Jones. Both my grandfather and father had seen T.G. in action and lauded his sublime talents. They claimed that he dribbled with the dazzling skills of Stanley Matthews, passed with the accuracy of Cliff Britton, tackled with the flawless timing of Joe Mercer, and headed the ball with the power of both Dean and Lawton, all while reading the game like, well, T.G. Jones. Younger fans may be unfamiliar with such stars, so let's say that his game embraced the best parts of Franz Beckenbauer, Alan Hansen, Paolo Maldini, Bobby Moore, Rio Ferdinand, and (dare I add) John Stones, who is known in our household as 'T.G. Stones'.

'The Uncrowned Prince of Wales' was something of an acquired taste. Used to no-nonsense defensive pivots who preferred to lump the ball (as well as the odd opponent) upfield, Goodison Park held its collective breath at the sight of

Jones gliding across his own box, executing the 1930s equivalent of Cruyff turns around the penalty spot before playing the ball through midfield. Apparently, his party piece had the stomachs of the Gwladys Street faithful in knots. At corners, he would cushion headers back to goalkeeper Ted Sagar.

I was sceptical about such nostalgia and solicited the opinions of the men who had walked in his giant footsteps. T.E. Jones, a centre-half who played over four hundred games for Everton between 1950 and 1961, told me: 'Imagine having the burden of following Tom Jones, especially with sharing the same first and last names? In my lifetime, he was the finest British defender to wear a number five shirt, and that includes his countryman John Charles.'

Next, I sought the counsel of Brian Labone, who had enjoyed more than five hundred games and great success between 1958 and 1971: 'By the late 50s I had become a first-team regular and the newspapers were referring to me as a future England international. I was brought down to earth by an old fan outside the Players' Entrance. After I had signed his autograph book, he looked me in the eye: "Young man, you may be a top-class centre-half but you'll never be as good as T.G."'

Finally, I quizzed someone who had played alongside him. Gordon Watson had been a teammate of Dean, won the title with Lawton and T.G., played wartime football with T.G., coached the first team containing Alex Young, and guided the development of youngsters such as Colin Harvey. My opening question was predictable: 'Was T.G. as comfortable on the ball as old-timers claim?' His response: 'Of course not – he was much better! He was refined. No, he was cultured. No, make that debonair!' And so I queried: 'Well, how come there is no statue of him at Goodison?' Then Gordon replied: 'Like Lawton, Mercer and the rest of the 1938/39 title-winning side, which was expected to dominate English football for a decade or more, his career was impacted by World War Two. Also, his standing was hindered by the fact that he hailed from the wrong side of Offa's Dyke. If he had been English, people would be talking about T.G.'s immense talents in hushed tones. Then there is the small matter of him not having a good word to say about the hierarchy at Everton Football Club.'

Intrigued, I visited the Bangor home of T.G. on several occasions – all of them memorable. Reluctantly, I must confirm that T.G. didn't share my love for all things blue, and had in fact boasted about walking away from Goodison in late 1949 to manage a Welsh League club and a hotel in Pwllheli. Clearly, he had not forgiven those responsible for his aborted move to AS Roma of Serie A. Instead of an astronomical signing-on bonus of £5,000, massive wages of £25 per week, a sun-drenched villa, new Lancia car, and first-class travel to and from Italy, the elegant defender settled for the maximum wage of £12 per week at Goodison before bolting to the home of Butlin's and Welsh nationalism, where – in his words – he enjoyed more respect and dodged playing in a poor Everton side destined for relegation. T.G. enjoyed chatting about representing Wales, but more than anything waxed lyrical about his belated Italian experience as manager of Bangor City in the early 60s. His team of part-timers, who played in the Cheshire League, had hammered AC Napoli of Serie A with a 2–0 victory in the European Cup Winners' Cup, before losing 3-1 to late goals in the second leg in Italy, and then 2–1 in the replay at Highbury.

Somewhere in royal blue heaven, my grandfather and father will be delighted that I've contributed to this volume about one of the unsung heroes of British football. Without question, T.G. Jones was an exceptional footballer whose elegance would have illuminated the playing fields of any era – especially those of the modern-day Premier League.

February 2016

FOREWORD

Kevin Ratcliffe

AS A FOOTBALLER I HAD THE HONOUR OF CAPTAINING BOTH my club and my country. My father made me aware that T.G. Jones, another son of Deeside, preceded me by forty years in those roles for Everton and Wales. T.G. set the benchmark against which Everton centre-halves such as T.E. Jones, Brian Labone, Roger Kenyon, Mark Higgins and myself were measured. If he were playing today, he would be a global star. But although revered on Merseyside and in North Wales, he has not received the wider acclaim that his performances deserved. I am delighted that Rob Sawyer has committed T.G.'s story to print so that future generations may appreciate one of the greatest talents to grace English and Welsh football.

INTRODUCTION

IF I WERE GIVEN THE KEYS TO A ROYAL BLUE TIME MACHINE, I would set the controls for Goodison Park, 5 May 1928. There I would join my grandfather and great-grandfather in watching William Ralph 'Dixie' Dean head his record-breaking sixtieth league goal in a season. I would, however, also make a couple of stops en route. First would be 19 August 1967, to see Harry Catterick's blossoming young side – boasting Colin Harvey, Howard Kendall and Alan Ball in midfield – demolish league champions Manchester United, with Alex Young scoring one of the most sublime Goodison goals. I would continue my journey via the autumn of 1938, to witness the Everton team that some maintain was the most deserving of the 'School of Science' tag. Alongside club legends such as Ted Sagar, Tommy Lawton and Joe Mercer, there was the jewel in the crown, a twenty-year-old centre-half called Thomas George Jones, better known to his adoring fans on Merseyside simply as 'T.G.'

In 2015, John Stones was beginning to display the hallmarks a thoroughbred centre-half. The young Yorkshireman had hearts in mouths as he pirouetted in his own penalty area, leaving opposing forwards in his wake before stroking the ball calmly to a teammate. Commentators were making comparisons with Alan Hansen and Rio Ferdinand, yet Evertonians of a certain vintage nodded sagely. They let their thoughts drift back seventy years, to an age when T.G. Jones bestrode Goodison Park with an air of supreme confidence that was matched by his ability, elegance and just a touch of arrogance. Dominant in the air and on the ground, his artistry enthralled and worried Toffees supporters in equal measure. In a fourteen-year career at the top, he delighted in being dubbed both 'The Prince of Centre-Halves' and 'The Uncrowned Prince of Wales'. T.G.'s level of skill and expertise was so great that Dixie Dean was adamant in naming him as the most complete footballer he had seen.

Jones hailed from the northeast corner of Wales, once known for its coal reserves, but also mined for its rich seam of footballing talent over the decades. Sons of this area, such as Billy Meredith, Roy Vernon, Mike England, Kevin Ratcliffe, Ian Rush, Mark Hughes and Gary Speed, would all go on to enjoy acclaim on the domestic and international stage. T.G. served his homeland with distinction, proudly captaining the national team on a number of occasions, and he stands alongside John Charles, Ian Rush and Gareth Bale as a genuine world-class talent to emerge from Wales. Off the pitch, he was handsome, smart, intelligent, eloquent, opinionated and, as he matured, a touch vain. With these impressive credentials, he should be an icon, and yet in recent decades T.G. has received scant recognition outside of Merseyside and North Wales, much less beyond these shores.

If T.G. had been born in 1997, rather than 1917, he could have become a global star. The camera would have adored him, but as he lived in a pre-television era, only a few glimpses of T.G. on flickering newsreels survive. In spite of all he accomplished, there remains a sense of underachievement and 'What if?'

What if he had not lost seven prime playing years to the Second World War? What if he had not suffered a career-threatening injury when aged 26? What if, with Everton in post-war decline, he had been granted a desired move to Arsenal, Manchester United – or even Roma, where he might have enjoyed Italian adulation a decade before John Charles? What if he had not walked away from professional football when still capable of gracing the Football League? What if T.G. had fully capitalised on the business, journalistic and managerial opportunities afforded him after his Everton days?

This is the bittersweet story of perhaps Britain and Everton's greatest ever centre-half, a man who was prepared to take on the football powers and ended up sacrificing his playing career to manage a hotel in North Wales. It encompasses a league title at Everton, leadership of the 'Invincibles' of Pwllheli Football Club, heady nights with Bangor City in European competition, and semi-retirement in relative obscurity while living above a newspaper shop.

More than anything, I hope this book gives you, the reader, a rounded insight into T.G., who merits all the recognition the publication may give him, a century after his birth.

EARLY YEARS

ALTHOUGH ONLY SEPARATED FROM ENGLAND BY THE RIVER
Dee, the Jones family were Welsh to the core. Residents for many generations in
and around Deeside, the men of the family had been employed in the maritime,
coal and steel industries. Thomas George Jones Sr and Elsie Plant had married
in Connah's Quay in 1917. Elsie had hailed from the Potteries, but her family had followed the well-trodden path from Staffordshire to work at Shotton
steelworks, the largest employer in the area.

With Thomas, a coal merchant by trade, away on duty as an Ordinary Seaman in the Royal Navy, Elsie awaited the birth of their first child at "Jericho",
her parent's house on Chester Road in Queensferry. The baby boy duly arrived
on 12 October 1917 and, as was customary, he was named after his father
and baptised 'Thomas George Ronald Jones'. In family circles he was known
as 'Tom', but throughout the football world he would come to be known as
'Tommy', or 'T.G.', after his first two initials. T.G. disliked his second middle
name, Ronald, and suffered much teasing for it at the hands of siblings and

cousins. In adult life he never made reference to it, and even his daughters were unaware of its existence.

Within months of the birth, the family relocated to Connah's Quay, initially living on Golftyn Lane and later in a terraced house in Pen Y Llan Street. T.G. was followed into the world in quick succession by four siblings: Bessie (1919), Jack (1921), Ellis (1923) and Ernest (1924). Sadly, Ernest, succumbing to illness, did not live to see his fifth birthday. A gifted sporting all-rounder with a lifelong love of swimming, the teenaged T.G. loved to swim across the River Dee – sometimes with his younger cousin Raynor Hawkes clinging to his back. Although T.G.'s father had no interest in football, his paternal grandfather, George Jones, was devoted to the sport, serving as chairman of Connah's Quay Football Club for fifteen years. A pillar of the local community, George also served as chorister at St Mark's Parish Church. In 2003, T.G. told Tony Coates of the Daily Post that his first recollections of watching football were of being taken to see Connah's Quay beat the Cardiff City team that had played at Wembley in the 1926 FA Cup final.

Aside from his grandfather, several others played a role in setting T.G. on the path to a football career. T.G.'s paternal aunt, Bessie (known as Auntie Bep), and her husband, David Bennett, were never blessed with children. Instead, they lavished time and love on their nieces and nephews. Bessie was a devout football follower, as T.G. recalled: 'An aunt of mine had put me into football – she was football mad. When I was a schoolboy she would take me watching Everton and Liverpool playing – so I knew what the clubs were.'[JR] A visit to Goodison Park with Bessie was T.G.'s first taste of First Division football, and he would even recount to author John Keith that he witnessed Dixie Dean score his record-breaking sixtieth league goal at the climax of the 1927/28 season (T.G. would only make this claim in an interview once). However, at this stage of his life, playing, rather than supporting a team, was everything: 'I didn't take any great interest in watching football until they took me to Wrexham. We didn't bother very much, as long as we were playing football it didn't matter. We played football in the streets or any patch of land – it was always a game of football. Sometimes it was a leather football – there wasn't much money around. If you had a pair of football boots you were a lucky lad.'[AS] Bessie, David and George would follow T.G.'s progress with interest, and attend all his home games once he broke through in professional football.

Another key influence on the bright youngster was an uncle, Jack Hawkes, well known on Deeside as a talented amateur footballer. His daughter, Raynor, recalls: 'Jack had been wounded in the calf during the First World War – every so often it opened up and pieces of shrapnel would come out. He was a very good footballer and played in the Cheshire League. Stoke and several other good clubs wanted him, but as head of a large family, he had to get a trade instead. He spent hours with Tommy – when he was a little lad – in a small backyard, teaching him what to do with a football.'

Although family members whetted T.G.'s appetite for the game, it was Baden Millington, a teacher at St Mark's School in Connah's Quay – just around the corner from the Jones household – who pushed him into playing competitively. T.G. stated in 1962: 'I was brought up in a keen football area. Instead of PE in school they threw us a football in the schoolyard and told us to get on with it. You may not believe it but I was sometimes reluctant to play soccer, but he [Baden Millington] would say to me, "You're playing football, and that's that!" I can't say if he ever spotted any real ability in me in those days but he certainly encouraged me a lot.' [WM]

Intriguingly, T.G. revealed in 2001 that his football career had almost followed a different path: 'I was a goalkeeper to start with at school and at nine or ten I got into the school first team in goal.'[JR] In the end, T.G.'s poise and skill convinced schoolmasters to switch him to the centre-half position.

During the early years of the twentieth century, the centre-half, or 'pivot' position, had been the fulcrum of a team – a deep-lying central midfielder in modern parlance, flanked by two wing-halves. Two full-backs would focus solely on defending while half-backs had responsibility for getting on the ball and distributing it to the five forwards. A change to the offside rule in 1925 had seen many teams, notably Herbert Chapman's successful Arsenal sides, dropping the central half-back role deeper. In this 'WM' formation, the centre-half position became, in effect, a third member of the defensive back-line, with a remit, primarily, to defend against the opposition's centre-forward. Few centre-halves – Jack Barker of Derby County and England being one exception – flew in the face of this 'stopper' convention and brought the ball forward regularly. T.G. certainly did not fit the new defensive template; he was loath to let defensive duties, superbly though he fulfilled them, nullify his creativity. In time, very few, if any, could match his ability to combine defensive excellence with playmaking intent.

Success on St Mark's School's playing fields led to T.G. captaining Flintshire Schoolboys, and at fourteen years of age he debuted at right-half for the national schoolboy side in two matches against their English counterparts. He commented: 'Under Mr Millington's tuition I was capped to play for Wales as a schoolboy, which was a rarity then in North Wales. I think I was the only North Walian playing in the team – they should have called it South Wales Schoolboys!'[AS]

Closer to home, T.G. kicked off the 1931/32 season with Primrose Hill FC in the newly formed Flintshire Amateur League. He remained there for three seasons while also turning out, on occasion, for Connah's Quay Amateurs. T.G. recalled: 'When I left school at fourteen I was a big strong lad and the only game I could get was in the men's league. At fifteen I was playing for Connah's Quay Amateurs when someone said, "Would you like to come for a trial at Wrexham?" [And] I thought: "Yes, that's marvellous." The thought of clubs like Everton and Liverpool was beyond chaps like us.'[AS]

Wrexham's manager, Ernest Blackburn, was sufficiently impressed by the trialist to take him on as an office boy and ground staff member at the Racecourse Ground, with amateur forms signed in May 1934: 'They signed me on and gave me a job doing an hour or two in the manager's office and training. They paid me a sizeable wage really – I couldn't believe it.' T.G. was permitted to continue playing for Connah's Quay Amateurs and, according to some accounts, Llanerch Celts – an outfit which served as an unofficial feeder club for Wrexham FC. Upon reaching the age of seventeen, the following October, T.G. was signed up as a professional at the Racecourse.

His first appearance for a Wrexham side came in a fundraising match to aid the bereaved of the Gresford Colliery disaster. On 22 September 1934, an explosion had ripped through the colliery near Wrexham, claiming the lives of 266 men and leaving 164 women widowed and 242 children without fathers. Wrexham, with T.G. debuting at centre-half, ran out 11–0 winners against Aberystwyth on Wednesday, 16 October. Ten days later, T.G. made his reserve-team debut in the Birmingham League, a 4–1 defeat to Worcester City.

After seeing T.G. make only his second appearance for the reserve team, in a 6–1 humbling of Stafford Rangers on 2 November, the Wrexham Leader's reporter, 'Robin', was already convinced that he had witnessed a player of extraordinary promise with an international future ahead of him.

His match report was remarkably perceptive:

> *In T.G. Jones, Wrexham have probably one of the most promising half-backs they have ever had on their books. Jones is only 17 years of age but his displays at centre-half in the reserve team's games… revealed that he possesses exceptional ability – so much so that his future progress will be interesting to note. He plays with the confidence and intelligence of a much older player. One admired the all-round cleverness of his display against Stafford. His headwork was always impressive and the way in which he varied his passing from wing to wing was another feature of his display. The effectiveness of Jones as pivot was one thing which stood out from the game.*

In spite of the positive impression made in those first matches, it would be months before T.G. became a regular in the reserve team. Key to T.G.'s football education in this period was a series of visits to Goodison Park, at Wrexham's behest, to watch Everton. The journalist Stork reflected on this in a 1938 article:

> *Wrexham sent him along to Goodison Park to see three games – Arsenal, Liverpool and Derby County – and Tommy says that was the turning point of his career. He was struck by the easy way Bradshaw, Barker, and Gee found their men and he decided that, if he was ever to become a top-class centre-half, he would have to master the art. Jones is a studious young man, and he was soon following in the footsteps of the great masters.[LE]*

In the summer of 1935, looking ahead to the approaching season, Robin repeated, in the Leader, his assertion that T.G. was destined for great things:

The club will be able to field a strong reserve side... including
one of the most promising young players on the club's books.
The player I refer to is T.G. Jones and it is not divulging any
secret when I say that many covetous eyes were cast upon him
last season. If last season's improvement is maintained his
future is assured.

With the onset of winter, reserve-team match reports indicated that T.G. was ready to make the step up to first-team football. After a 5–1 defeat of Dudley on 7 December 1935, the Leader singled T.G. out for further praise: 'Jones' splendid play at centre-half was responsible for much of the side's success. He was as enterprising in attack as he was resourceful in defence with a splendid goal rounding off a capital performance at centre-half.'

T.G.'s first-team bow duly came on 28 December when Ernest Blackburn selected him to debut in the royal blue shirt of Wrexham (the club would not switch to a more patriotic red strip until 1939) against Rotherham at the Racecourse Ground. T.G. helped his team keep a clean sheet in a 2–0 victory watched by 3,500 spectators. 'XYZ', reporting on the match for the Leader, commented: 'T.G. Jones was creating a very favourable impression upon his first appearance.'

T.G. would retain his place for a further five matches. In only his third game, he played in front of 10,000 people in a 1–1 draw with local rivals Chester at Sealand Road. The derby, described by the local press as 'literally packed with thrills', saw Wrexham soak up much Chester pressure. T.G. was described as having 'shone' and 'tackled so surely'. He recalled the match in 1962: 'I played eight or nine times [sic] for the first team and one of my sternest feats at that tender age was to play in a local derby against Chester – quite an experience for a youngster! But I was really too young for Wrexham's first team and played mainly in the Birmingham League team.'[WM]

His sixth and, as it transpired, final Football League appearance for Wrexham, on 7 March 1936, saw him contribute to another clean sheet in a victory over York City. The Leader reported:

T.G. Jones came back into the side and gave another promis-
ing exhibition. His inches are valuable and his ability to
glide the ball to colleagues is a feature of his play. He is

a player who should develop into a first-class pivot. I am sure that Mr Jack Sharp and Mr Gibbins of the Everton club, who were at Wrexham on Saturday, must have been delighted with his skilful handling of the ball.

The two Everton directors were in the stand with a specific remit to run the rule over the prodigiously talented eighteen-year-old. Their scouting mission was given urgency by rumours of interest from Aston Villa and Birmingham City. It was becoming clear that T.G.'s days at the Racecourse Ground were already numbered.

2

EVERTON CALLING

UNTIL THE POST-WAR YEARS EVERTON FOOTBALL CLUB DID
not have a team manager. Training the first team was a job left to Harry Cooke,
whose association with the club as player and coach went back to 1904. Tactical
decisions were largely the preserve of senior professionals in the squad such as
the captain Dixie Dean and his vice-captain Jock Thomson. Team selection and
transfer activity was the domain of the club's directorate, with some input from
club secretary Theo Kelly. Kelly, the son of sports journalist Louis T. Kelly (writing as Stud Marks) had been promoted to the role in February 1936 upon the
death of the incumbent Tom McIntosh from cancer.

Having assessed T.G.'s performance against York at close quarters, Messrs
Sharp and Gibbins reported back to their fellow Everton directors that the
centre-half was 'an extremely promising player'(BM). It was agreed to offer
Wrexham up to £1,500 for T.G.'s transfer, with an opening bid of £1,250 to
be tabled. In the end, £1,400 was enough to persuade Wrexham to do business
(erroneously, a figure double that was reported in some press articles). A switch

to Everton was not a foregone conclusion, however. Aston Villa's centre-half, Tom Griffiths, nudged his club to match Everton's offer to the Wrexham board. T.G. recalled how his manager, Ernest Blackburn, himself a former Aston Villa player, gave him a choice: 'The manager called me into the office one day and he said, "Look here, two clubs want you to move. We don't want you to go but we've got to get rid of you; we've got to get some money from somewhere to pay the summer wages." I didn't want to go, I loved Wrexham. The two clubs who were interested were Aston Villa… and Everton… I took the manager's advice. He said, "Everton, because it's close to home," so I went to Everton.'[RT]

T.G. gave a slightly different slant on his decision-making process to George Lerry in 1962: 'There were several First Division clubs that I could have joined. I fancied Aston Villa but Tommy Griffiths was already filling the Villa's first-team centre-half position so what chance had I?'[WM]

Griffiths was another one in a line of great centre-halves that Wales would produce. The teenaged T.G., eleven years Griffiths' junior, had idolised the older man. Griffiths, like T.G., started out at Wrexham before progressing to Everton, where he spent five-and-a-half seasons, winning international honours along the way. Dislodged from the Everton first team in 1931, Griffiths went on to play for Bolton Wanderers and Middlesbrough before moving to Aston Villa.

So, it appears that a combination of Goodison Park's proximity to T.G.'s home in Connah's Quay and the more immediate prospect of first-team action was enough to tip the balance in the Toffees' favour. The deal was sealed by 11 March, with wages set at £5 per week, and an additional £1 bonus when selected for the first team. T.G. recalled that his signing-on bonus was substantial for the time: 'I signed on for £250, which was a lot of money back then. In those days that was enough to buy a house.'[JR]

Ernest Blackburn, on seeing his protégé leave Wrexham, told the press: 'He should be a world-beater in a season or two.'[EP] T.G. continued to train midweek with Wrexham for the remainder of the season, travelling to Merseyside only on match days. He would move to live in the city in time for the start of the 1936/37 season.

The departure of the teenager caused apoplexy among Wrexham fans, and an extraordinary general meeting was called at the Mine Workers' Institute. The club chairman, John Hughes, gave a statement in which he outlined the club's financial plight and the necessity to cash in so early in T.G.'s career:

> *The board were [sic] unanimous in agreeing to Everton's terms for this player. This transfer, the second one of the season, has again been necessary to put the club financially sound, which will again contradict the rumours flying around that a few directors who are resigning are deserting a sinking ship. The only alternative I see to the transfer of players is for the shareholders to endeavour to find a sporting gentleman, two or three if possible, who will back the club to the tune of at least £5,000 which might then help to obtain Second Division football.*

As it was, Wrexham remained rooted in the Third Division North until the creation of a national Third Division in 1958.

Having chosen Everton, T.G. was wide-eyed at the prospect of joining a club of such stature. In 1992, he reflected: 'I was full of ambition, and I wanted to see things, and I looked forward to it tremendously. Mixing with all the players, great names... it was marvellous actually. I used to look with great respect to these players who were at Everton. I used to think, "My God, what an honour." I would go back and tell my parents and my friends. They would look at me and want to hear all about it because going to a football match from Connah's Quay was an event.'[RT]

T.G.'s transfer to Merseyside coincided with that of another great name in British football as Matt Busby, then a half-back, moved to Liverpool from Manchester City. Joining T.G. at Goodison Park's entrance door was Tranmere's Robert 'Bunny' Bell, a prolific striker brought in as back-up for the increasingly injury-prone Dixie Dean.

The belief of T.G. that first-team opportunities would come sooner on Merseyside than at Villa Park may have been misguided. Barring his progression to the Goodison senior ranks were two English international 'pivots' in Charlie Gee and Tommy White. Gee was a commanding centre-half in the classical 'stopper' tradition, whose meteoric rise had not been unlike T.G.'s. After less than a season of appearances for his home-town club Stockport County in the Third Division North, he was snapped up by freshly relegated Everton in 1930. Within half a season, he had dislodged the teenage T.G.'s footballing idol, Tom Griffiths, from the first team, and won Second and First Division championship medals in successive seasons. Gee had also won England honours on two occasions but missed out on the 1933 FA Cup triumph due to a chronic knee injury suffered in 1932. He had never quite regained the level of mobility he enjoyed before the injury but, turning 27 in April 1936, he was still in his prime years and a formidable opponent for any centre-forward. Off the field, Gee was a larger-than-life character – adept as a raconteur and 'choirmaster' at squad social events. On seeing T.G. train for the first time, he was reported to have commented to team-mates that his days at Everton were numbered.

The Lancastrian Tommy White was a versatile player who was comfortable at centre-half or centre-forward, and he often deputised for Dixie Dean during his injury lay-offs. At the time of T.G.'s arrival from Wrexham, White was holding down the centre-half position in the first team. T.G. would have to be content in the short term with life in the Central League (reserve) team. He and Bob Bell debuted for the second string in an away defeat to Oldham Athletic on 14 March. T.G. recalled the trepidation he felt playing alongside household names: 'Their reserve side was frightening to me... Warney Cresswell was left-back. Cliff Britton was right-half and they put me in at centre-half. There were seven or eight full internationals in the reserve side.'[RT]

Cresswell, a veteran of two league title wins and an FA Cup victory with Everton, was then in his thirty-ninth year and approaching the end of his fruitful association with the Toffees. His positional nous and ability to jockey opposing forwards without resorting to rash challenges was so revered that he had been dubbed 'The Prince of Full-Backs'. Teammate Ted Sagar described him thus in an Everton programme article from 1969: 'Warney was the most stylish back I ever played behind. He was a brilliant reader of the game and always put himself in a position to make things look easy.' The teenaged T.G. could not have failed, at close quarters, to be impressed and influenced by the north-easterner's approach to the game. It is perhaps no coincidence that, in time, T.G. would exude the same positional awareness and come to be known by supporters as 'The Prince of Centre-Halves'. Looking back in 1990, for an Everton match-day programme article, T.G. recalled what it was like training and playing alongside household names: 'To say I was overawed is an understatement but I learned a lot from them. If I made a mistake they came down on me like a ton of bricks. And if I made two I was in big trouble.'

In spite of any butterflies experienced, T.G.'s home debut for the second string, against Birmingham City reserves on 21 March, was triumphant. Bell hit a hat-trick while T.G. was praised in the Liverpool Daily Post for his 'fine constructive and defensive work'. Louis T. Kelly, father of Everton's secretary Theo Kelly, used his 'Stud Marks' column in the Liverpool Football Echo to state: 'First impressions of Everton's latest centre-half recruit, Jones of Wrexham, are that he is "the goods".'

For many Everton supporters, a first, low-key, sighting of T.G. occurred at Goodison Park in the annual Blues versus Whites trial match prior to the 1936/37 season. These matches, open to the public, pitted the expected first team (Blues) against the second string (Whites). With first-team places at stake for the approaching season these matches were fiercely contested. Bee reported favourably on the newcomer:

> *T.G. Jones of Wrexham made a welcome appearance in the second half in place of White. He is a very tall boy, has youth on his side, and he got a warm welcome from those who recognised the newcomer, but there were not many who realised who the newcomer was... Jones, centre-half, in the little time that he was on the field, made a good impression by his coolness and wise use of the ball and also with a flashing shot.* (DP)

Having impressed in the first trial match, and with Tom White injured, T.G. was elevated to the Blues team for the second trial match staged five days later. Pilot noted in the Echo beforehand: 'T.G. Jones, the young Wrexham lad, plays in the Blues' side for White, and his form will be watched with interest. Jones showed up well during the second half of last Monday's trial when he came on to deputise for White. He is a player of great promise.'(EE)

He did not disappoint, serving notice of his ability in attack and defence:

> *The best goal of the day was that scored by T. Jones, ex-Wrexham, who from a longish distance shot with such ter-*

rific force that the goalkeeper could not have had a sight of the ball. This boy has the making of a good pivot because he is not inclined to third back principles and his height leads him to many a ball he could not otherwise get. Best of all he has a strong inclination to start combined movements rather than merely getting rid of the ball.[(DP)]

Based on such promising performances in the trial matches there was speculation that T.G. might be blooded in the 1936/37 season's curtain-raiser at Highbury. In the event Charlie Gee's experience was preferred, T.G. instead playing alongside Jock Thomson for the reserves at Goodison against Preston North End. His display in a 2–0 win was described as 'prominent'.[(DP)] A 4–2 win over Burnley reserves gave T.G. ample opportunity to demonstrate his aerial dominance and free-kick technique: 'But for some stern work by Jones (T) at centre-half, the steady flow of the centres which came across the Everton goalmouth would have taken greater toll... Finally a free kick for an offside that was not clear to most people led to Jones (TG) scoring with a magnificent shot to round off an unusually interesting mid-week match.'[(DP)]

A senior call-up seemed increasingly likely, and it came after Charlie Gee received a one-match suspension for head-butting a Wolves player. The England international had to sit out the following Saturday's fixture away to Leeds United on 17 October. The Everton team selected was: Ted Sagar, George Jackson, Billy Cook, Cliff Britton, T.G. Jones, Joe Mercer, Albert Geldard, Torry Gillick, Bill 'Dixie' Dean (captain), Alex Stevenson, Charlie Leyfield. The match ended in a 3–0 defeat, of which T.G. recalled: 'Dixie was centre-forward – we got murdered!'[(JR)] On a wet, sticky pitch the teenager came close to marking his debut with a long-range goal. The Football Echo's Bee reported: 'From thirty yards' range Jones made the first Everton shot of the day, and would have scored his maiden goal on his debut if McInroy had not produced a magnificent save which sent the ball over the bar.'

T.G. would go on to get his name on the scoresheet at Elland Road but, for the first of numerous times over his career, it was in the wrong net. Bee described T.G.'s misfortune: 'Hyde's shot cannoned off the outstretched leg of Jones and in past the helpless Ted Sagar to put Leeds three goals to the good. Sagar threw his cap to the ground in disgust.' Scoreline notwithstanding, Bee was still impressed with the debutant:

> *Jones, ex-Wrexham, was making his debut for Everton's first team, and the tall young pivot, aged but nineteen, showed up in many ways as a centre half-back of understanding. He is not a resolute or deadly tackler till he gets his long legs in a double-footed stabbing effort. Yet he has splendid points in the matter of attack and a graceful movement as well. His method of taking the ball up and swinging it to the wings was ideal, and the time came when he let go his famous long shot drive which McInroy did really well to stop with a magnificent save which sent the ball over the bar.*

In another column, written post-match, Bee's praise was counterbalanced by some constructive criticism:

> *Everton gave birth to the new centre half-back of Wrexham, Jones by name, and as unlike Griffiths as ever you saw! Same in height as near as no matter, nineteen years old, stately framed and football minded; able to give the wingers passes, and altogether a gem in attack, needing the defending vein which does not come easily to these nonchalant-looking pivots. He would use the ball, but it had to come to him from the loose. His heading was good and his general demeanour praiseworthy. It is good to see the promise of a boy of this character.*

T.G. was distracted, during his debut, by the gulf between lower league and reserve team football and the First Division, as a press cutting reported: 'Willis Edwards nearly took me off my own game. I was so fascinated by his wonderful ball play. His deft touches to his inside and wing-men and the way he took up positions made me stop and watch him! Edwards was making the ball do as much work with one touch as I'd seen many Third Division players do in three.' The following week, Charlie Gee was back in the side and T.G. returned to the second string for the remainder of the season. There, he continued to learn his trade in a team brimming with talent. Notable names to appear alongside him were Jackie Coulter, Charlie Leyfield, Gordon Watson, Stan Bentham and Albert Geldard. In later life, T.G. was sparing in his praise for former teammates, but he readily acknowledged that Watson and Cliff Britton were the best passers of a ball he had ever encountered. Coulter, the dazzling Irish outside-left, was rated by T.G. as the most skilful dribbler he had seen.

Although the vast majority of his playing career was spent at centre-half, T.G. was always confident of his ability to operate higher up the pitch – as another great Welsh centre-half, John Charles, would do in the 1950s. During his first full season at Everton it appears that a concerted effort was made to convert him into an inside-forward in the reserve team. In November 1936, when turning out at inside-left forward for the first time, he garnered a rave review from Bee:

> *On Saturday there was an inside-left playing against Shef-*
> *field United reserves, at Goodison Park, who was voted by*
> *everyone as 'the best forward on the field' – and the name*
> *is Jones (T.G.). Popular players like Coulter and Geldard*
> *of Everton, and Settle and McPherson of Sheffield, were*
> *overshadowed by the fine display of T.G. Jones who was play-*
> *ing his first game as an Everton forward. He added fire and*
> *direction to the attack, encouraging the Everton forwards to*
> *give one of the most forceful displays of the season. His strong*
> *kicking and accurate passes were a feature of the game, mak-*
> *ing many openings for his colleagues, and on several occasions*
> *almost scoring himself with terrific drives from long range.* [LE]

T.G. would spend much of the season in the reserve team's inside-right position alongside the quicksilver right-winger Albert Geldard, who had been displaced from the first team by Torry Gillick. He recounted what it was like playing with Geldard, one of the fastest players in the business: 'They put me to play inside-forward. I used to go up for corners and free kicks and Theo Kelly decided to put me at inside-right because I was scoring a few goals. Albert was so very, very, quick – God, he could go! You had to slip them in to him. I used to get the ball and push it inside the full-back and Albert was gone – they couldn't catch him. I have never seen a player faster than Albert, and he could score goals too.'[JR]

Although T.G. was progressing in the reserve team, off the field the transition from the familiarity and security of Connah's Quay to living in a club-owned house on Walton Hall Avenue was proving to be problematic. In 1992, he was candid about the mental struggles which threatened to curtail an Everton career still in its infancy: 'I found the environment totally different. Quite honestly, for the first twelve months I found it difficult to live in Liverpool. For a while my health suffered a bit and I do know that at the end of the season they were on the verge of letting me go… because of my health. I was totally run down and the suggestion was made then that I go to live at home… which I did, and of course I grew tremendously then… I think [becoming ill] was [due to] going to a big city from a village.'[RT]

Once resettled across the Welsh border, back in the family home, T.G. was in a better place, psychologically, to push for a regular place in the first team. He would later recall his journey from Connah's Quay to the ground on match days: 'When I was living at home I'd catch a train through to Seacombe, catch the ferry across the river and catch the number twenty-two tram – I still remember the number – up to Walton. There were always discussions going on, on the tram. Very often people would be travelling from home; they'd come with me all the way. You didn't need to be at the ground till half an hour before the kick-off, and even after that some players would stroll in. Half an hour before the kick-off was plenty of time, just to get changed, because the day before you'd discussed most of [the tactics].'[RT]

T.G. spent the early stages of the 1937/38 season in the reserve side alongside Dixie Dean. According to T.G., Dean lobbied Theo Kelly for the Welshman's elevation to the first team. After fourteen reserve appearances, a second senior call-up came about in the autumn. The first team was in a poor run of form, and after a 3–5 reverse to Preston North End at Goodison Park discontented supporters milled around after the match, chanting at the directors: 'We want some players – we want Dean!' Dean had made a rare appearance in the previous match – a defeat to Grimsby – before making way, again, for Tommy Lawton. Relegated to the reserves he would only be selected once more for the first team – failing to score in his swansong against Birmingham City on 11 December.

Charlie Gee found himself to be the fall guy, and T.G. started for the Blues at Ayresome Park on 6 November, when Tommy Lawton's brace secured victory over Middlesbrough. T.G.'s sole lapse allowed Middlesbrough in to score but the Liverpool Football Echo's Stork highlighted the supreme confidence in dangerous situations, which would become the Welshman's hallmark:

Jones had made a good impression, even though he had put our hearts in our mouths when he elected to trap a ball in front of his own goal when there were several Borough men in the vicinity. He got away with it and also got away with many headers which, had they been allowed to pass along, would have been dangerous to the Everton goal.

There was great speculation as to how T.G. Jones would fare in this severe test. Well sirs, he came through with flying colours. His defence was sound, his use of the ball wise and it was regrettable that his one mistake – if it could be adjudged a mistake – would cost his side a goal. Jones brought his wing halves into the game, and Mercer and Britton gave him strong backing. This line was partly responsible for the victory.

Many Everton supporters caught their first glimpse of T.G. at Goodison Park the following week. Lawton fired another double as Chelsea were trounced 4–1. Comments by the Merseyside press corps on T.G.'s home debutant were universally positive. Stork (Daily Post) noted: 'T.G. Jones kept a firm hand on Mills in his quiet, yet confident way, and had an eye to the attack. Jones and Cook defended splendidly.' In the Evening Express, 'Watcher' concurred with Stork's assessment: 'Jones (T.G.); the former Wrexham pivot was the personification of coolness, and consequently, Mills had little chance.'

An away defeat at the Hawthorns followed, but Stork noted the constructive nature of T.G.'s play: 'Jones played the "policeman" à la Roberts, but he did more than that; he utilised his wing half-backs when clearing. No haphazard kicking with the chance of the ball going to an opponent and coming back to put further work on his shoulders.'[FE] And there was also praise in defeat from Pilot: 'Tom Jones, who gave another brilliant display at centre-half, was the outstanding man of the side. He rarely left Richardson for a second.'[EE]

It was rapidly becoming apparent that T.G. could bring a new dimension to the Everton team. No matter what the situation, he showed a remarkable calmness when in possession of the ball which defied his tender years. This was allied to his dominance in the air and sparing use of his great kicking power, preferring to constructively pass the ball to the inside-forwards. Such was T.G.'s level of performance that the more stylistically orthodox Gee, who had been capped as recently as November 1936, would henceforth only appear for the first team sporadically.

Gee was not alone in finding his place under threat. Against a backdrop of possible relegation, the directors dropped established stars such as Jackie Coulter, Albert Geldard and Cliff Britton in search of a winning formula. The most notable casualty of the changing of the guard was Dixie Dean. As the 1937/38 season got under way, Dean's all-round play, if not his unparalleled heading ability, was increasingly compromised by the cumulative effect of injuries. In contrast to Dean, T.G. was in peak shape and able to dominate and frustrate the forward on the ground and in aerial duels during training and practice matches. Nevertheless, T.G. recalled the awe in which he held Dean and the influence the club captain exerted: 'Dixie Dean was Everton. Make no mistake about that. I was an innocent lad, you see, and he was the man who almost picked the team on his own. The story was that he used to go up to the office and say, "This is the team we're playing [fielding] on Saturday." I don't know whether it's true or not but that was the story.'[RT]

This state of affairs meant that Dean threatened the authority of Theo Kelly. Kelly's predecessor as club secretary, the avuncular Tom McIntosh, had been instrumental in securing Dean's transfer from Tranmere in 1925 and the two formed had a close bond. According to Dean's biographer, Nick Walsh, this was close to a father-son relationship and there is reasonable to assume that the striker would have had the ear of McIntosh in matters of team selection. Kelly, however was prepared to challenge the talismanic, but declining, centre-forward. The stance taken by Kelly was unpopular with supporters, in light of the esteem in which Dean was still held by them. First, the secretary had to identify and recruit a worthy replacement for Dean – no easy task. He duly arrived, in December 1936, in the shape of Tommy Lawton – Burnley's Farnworth-born prodigy. Seventeen-year-old Lawton usurped Dean in the first team after a brief bedding-in period in the reserves. T.G. would come to revere Lawton just as he had Dean. After Lawton's death in 1996, a clearly emotional T.G. stated: 'Tommy was the complete centre-forward – two very good feet, strong in the air and quick with a great understanding of the game.'[DP]

Debate among Evertonians has raged as to which of the two centre-forward icons was the greatest. T.G. himself was generally noncommittal on the subject, but when pressed for an opinion upon Lawton's death, he eventually erred towards the younger man: '[Lawton and Dean] were equals and both very, very good but in different ways. Dixie was great in the air – that's how he scored most of his goals. Tommy was not as good at that but he was better on the ground and he was a big strong fellow. Possibly he was the best.'[DP]

Dean's Everton first-team career was effectively over by September 1937, as Lawton's bountiful goal haul made the battle-scarred veteran surplus to requirements. After six months in the reserves, Dean was unceremoniously shipped out to Notts County, leaving him stuck on 399 league appearances for the Toffees. Troubled by ankle injuries, he subsequently wound down his playing career at Sligo Rovers in Ireland and non-league Hurst FC before retiring upon the outbreak of war. He had played in only two first-team games alongside T.G., the first being the Welshman's debut at Leeds in October 1936, the second being his own Goodison Park swansong in December 1937. The pair did line up together numerous times in the reserve side, however. In 1977, when asked by author John Roberts to name the greatest player he ever saw, Dean did not hesitate in his answer: 'He would have to be an Evertonian: T.G. Jones, the Welsh international centre-half. The best all-round player I've ever seen. He had everything – no coach could ever teach him anything. He was neater than John Charles. John looked awkward whereas Tommy would get out of a ruck by just opening his legs, letting the ball run wide and all this sort of thing – just letting it run through.'

CHAMPIONS

IN SPITE OF THE GLOOM ENVELOPING THE GOODISON terraces in the winter of 1937, green shoots had become apparent towards the end of the season which saw Everton finish just three points above the relegation places. Aside from Tommy Lawton, astute signings had been made in the form of West Bromwich Albion's England international left-winger, Wally Boyes, and New Brighton's full-back, Norman Greenhalgh. Meanwhile, the two Tommies – Lawton and Jones – were fast developing into First Division stars. T.G. was rewarded with a call-up to the Welsh team that played Ireland at Windsor Park on 16 March. On the opposition side were Everton teammates Billy Cook, Jackie Coulter and Alex Stevenson. Sitting in the corner of the changing room as kick-off approached, T.G. was approached by his predecessor and boyhood hero, Tom Griffiths, who was acting as an unofficial advisor to the squad. T.G. was given 'a few words of advice and encouragement'. He would later enthuse: 'What a thrill those few words gave me. I'll never forget it.'

Although buoyed by his unexpected pep talk, T.G. experienced butterflies as the teams stood for the national anthems, but settled into the match and soon recovered his composure: 'When we lined up I didn't know whether I was on my head or my heels. Once the whistle was blown I was calm enough. Although I wasn't a flop I did nothing to crow about. I'll always look back on the game with pleasure, though – because of the Griffiths touch.' In the early exchanges T.G.'s challenge on the inside-forward Paddy Farrell reduced the Irish contingent to ten men. The Dundee Courier reported: 'The work of the Welsh halves was grand, T.G. Jones dominating the centre of the field...' Stork, on the other hand, felt that T.G. had not asserted himself fully in the 1–0 defeat: 'In his first national, Jones did not quite satisfy because of his quiet demeanour. It was something new to the Welshman. He will do just the same thing as Keenor and Griffiths did, but in a much more gentle manner. He will dominate without appearing to do so.'[LE]

In spite of the promising signs, few would have predicted that within a year Everton would be crowned champions of England. T.G. partly attributed the jump in performance to the catalyst provided by Everton's post-season participation in the Empire Exhibition Cup. The competition, held in Glasgow in June 1938, saw Everton advance to the final in front of 82,000 at Ibrox – losing by a solitary goal in extra time. T.G. recalled to Rogan Taylor: 'We went to Glasgow for a couple of weeks... and all the top Scottish teams were there and one or two English teams. And we got to the final... Glasgow Celtic beat us. It did something for us, that competition, because the next year we walked away with the First Division.' Tommy Lawton endorsed T.G.'s view: 'That is where we got our act together – because of five-a-sides, comradeship and friendship.'[RT] The invaluable experience of playing quality opponents in front of fervent Glaswegian support was complemented by trips to Arran and Dunoon and evenings spent at the likes of the Barrfields Pavilion in Largs. These shared experiences fostered a sense of togetherness which would stand the squad in good stead in the months to come.

The bond grew particularly strong between T.G., Tommy Lawton and Joe Mercer, both of whom both called the Welshman 'Tom'. T.G. and Lawton became inseparable, as teammate Gordon Watson recalled: 'They were room-mates wherever they went. They always dressed smartly. When they went out it looked as if they were going to church! They were very nice lads, hardly ever swore and never drank.'[RT] Although a taste for alcohol may have come later, the pair were, already, more than capable of getting involved in high jinks on away trips, with the two Tommies being both the instigators and victims of pranks. One such episode, during an overnight stay in Dorking before a January 1938 fixture against Brentford, was recounted in Lawton's autobiography, Football Is My Business:

> *I was sharing a room with Tom Jones and we had retired for the night and were yawning in bed when Tom suddenly said, 'Shush, can you hear what I can hear?' I could, it was a slow knocking on the wall... suddenly there was an outburst of whispering and then a high-pitched scream. Without more ado both Tom and I dived for the door, and, convinced the room was haunted, spent the night huddled round a huge fire in the hall... At breakfast we were told, amongst roars of laughter from the rest of the crowd, that Norman Greenhalgh, Wally Boyes and Alex Stevenson had found a secret passage in this rather old-fashioned hotel and they were the 'ghosts'. Tom and I weren't allowed to forget the 'haunting' all day long.*

Pilot would note: '[T.G.] is the butt of the boys, who are always chipping him, but he stands up to them just as effectively as he does to centre-forwards.'[LE] Sure enough, revenge was sought on this occasion, but with the perpetrators keeping their room doors securely locked, it was the sleeping Torry Gillick who fell victim to a 'blood-curdling howl' emitted by the two Tommies. According to Lawton, the Scot exited his bedroom at 'Olympic Games sprint pace... muttering fierce Gaelic oaths'.

T.G. recalled how the tide turned as the 1938/39 season got under way: 'The year before we won the league, Everton were in a mess and had a job to escape relegation. They brought a lot of young players into the team for the following season: me, Norman Greenhalgh from New Brighton; George Jackson was right-back; Torry Gillick, Joe Mercer, Tommy Lawton and Stan Bentham. Alex Stevenson was inside-left. We were a good side with a lot of young players.'[JR] The season started with two victories and no goals conceded, prompting Stork to comment:

> *Everton are on top of the world – two games played, both*

won, five goals for and none against. The last note is the most pleasing of all, for it shows stiffening up where it was most required – in defence. Tom Jones was classic in all his work, and particularly in his use of the ball, and on his flanks Mercer and Thomson worked zealously and thoughtfully throughout. Thomson's capacity for work was astonishing. [EE]

In the fourth game of the season Aston Villa were swept aside 3–0 by Everton on their own turf in one of the great performances of the season. Pilot witnessed the 'thrilling team work':

Tom Jones was the big man in defence; the acme of cool, concentrated breaking up and diligent use of the ball. On current form there is no better pivot in the land. Behind him was the 'reliability trio' – Sagar, Cook and Greenhalgh. On his flanks were Mercer, who, by the way, has a perfect understanding with Cook these days, making for vast improvement in the rear-guard; and Thomson, who was quick on the ball, strong in the tackle. Both were artistic in their distribution. [EE]

More than twenty years later, the journalist Peter Morris eloquently reflected, for Charles Buchan's Football Monthly, on this match and a team which some older Evertonians maintain was more 'scientific' than the title-winning sides of the late 1960s and mid-1980s:

Perhaps you could put it down to nostalgia… nostalgia for a crisp, smoky September evening back in 1938 when I saw an Everton team give the finest all-round club performance in my memory. There was no thought of Hitler or his Nazi legions in the thoughts of myself and the 40,000 spectators packed tightly on the terraces of Villa Park that evening. We watched that wonderful Everton side coast to a 3–0 win over Villa with a brand of soccer that, even now, after 22 years, has lost none of its sweetness. Since the war I have admired the 'push and run' of Spurs, the colourful, inspired football of Manchester United and the ruthless power play of Wolves.

> *But none has recaptured for me the sheer magic of that*
> *Everton team… Everton had the stars to match the poetry of*
> *football in that last autumn of peace.*

The next fixture promised to be another stern test when Everton travelled to Highbury to take on the reigning league champions, Arsenal. During a pre-match training camp at a luxury hotel in Bushey, Harry Cooke issued rubber training shoes to the squad in order to encourage pace.

Since the Scottish tournament, the focus in training had veered towards six-a-side matches where fast, one-touch passing play was paramount. This slick style of play allowed Everton to overcome Arsenal, with Lawton continuing his hot scoring streak – he scored in each of the first six games of the season. John Macadam of the Daily Express was impressed with the Highbury display, writing: 'This was vintage football. Cool, deliberate, rhythmic and planned. Every man on the Everton side had a duty to that ball – to play, no matter what the risk… the ball was handled like a weakly child – wheedled, guided, fed and occasionally belted.'

After this flying start to the season, the team would never drop below second place in the table. T.G. prided himself that it was November before a centre-forward scored past him in open play.

Breaking through to the senior team around the same time as T.G. was Gordon Watson, a wing-half hailing from Blyth Spartans. He would play alongside T.G. before, during and after the Second World War, affording him an unrivalled footballing insight into the Welshman. 'T.G. was the best signing that Everton ever made,'[RT] he insisted. Watson dubbed T.G. 'Cryogenic Jones' in recognition of his teammate's unflappable, cool demeanour on the pitch. He considered the centre-half, who was three years his junior, to be level-headed and serious for his tender years. When reflecting with author David France in 1999, Watson put T.G. in the same bracket as Franz Beckenbauer – the German who captained his national team to World Cup success in 1974. In Watson's opinion, no other player – before or after – had come close to exhibiting the intelligence, ball skills and composure of T.G.

Fifty years after establishing himself in Everton's first team, T.G. ruminated on his penchant for bringing the ball out from defence: 'I developed this ability to be able to kill the ball, then bring it under control and beat people by dribbling. Many times I'd bring the ball down dead in the penalty box and then, with a shrug of the shoulders, I'd have two or three people going the other way. Don't ask me how or why – it was sheer instinct. The brain couldn't work quick enough to think about it – you did it instinctively. Today they'd call it talent, I suppose.'[AS]

In the British Championship match held on 22 October 1938 at Cardiff's Ninian Park, T.G. made his second appearance for the national team. On the opposing side was England debutant Tommy Lawton. Ranger reported on the friendly rivalry: 'At Bolton, on Saturday, Lawton "promised" Jones that if they were both chosen he would pop in at least one goal against Wales, to which Jones jokingly replied that no centre-forward this season had scored against him, and Lawton wasn't going to be the first to break the ice.'[FE]

Wales ran out 4–2 winners, with T.G. keeping the England centre-forward on a tight leash. Lawton recalled exclaiming to T.G. during the match, 'Blimey you're a hard bugger,' to which T.G. responded: 'What do you expect? Your shirt's the wrong colour today!' George Lerry's match report noted: 'Lawton found his way to the Welsh goal bolted and barred.'[WM]

Although, geographically, T.G. only just qualified as a Welshman, he was proud of his nationality. John Ogwen, who played for T.G. in Bangor City's reserve team in the early 1960s, recalls: 'It was the last match of the Welsh League season and we had played Nantlle Vale. Tommy actually played in baseball boots! We were in the Eagles pub in Caernarfon afterwards and, as a sixteen-year-old, [I] was just allowed one bottle of very light ale. Tommy had his leg pulled by Freddie Pye, the manager of Nantlle Vale FC, that he could pee farther than the distance Tommy was born from the English border.' Incandescent at the slight on his Welshness, T.G. had delved into his wallet and brandished a yellowing copy of the match report from that 1938 Ninian Park match. Point made.

Ted Sagar, keeping goal behind T.G. in the title-winning season, was a veteran of nine seasons on Merseyside and an England international. In 1938, at the age of 28, he was in his prime. Referred to as 'The Boss' by teammates, this acknowledged not only his ability but also his proclivity for giving his teammates both barrels if they erred, as Gordon Watson recalled: 'Nine times out of ten Ted Sagar would play merry hell with you if you passed the ball back to him. He used to say: "I've got enough to do watching these fellows as well as passing back from our own players."'[RT]

As part of the team's spine, it was imperative that T.G. and Sagar had a sound understanding of each other's methods. In 1970, T.G. reflected on their relationship on and off the pitch: 'I think some of the moves we used were twenty years ahead of our time. It was mainly due to the confidence Ted and I had in each other.'[EP] Although friendly during their post-playing days, there was often an underlying tension between T.G. and Sagar as players. T.G. recalled: 'It was strange, you know, Ted and I didn't really get on with each other off the pitch. Although we are great friends now, there seemed to be some antagonism between us in those days.'[EP]

T.G. elaborated on the friction when he looked back with David France in 1999, confiding that he had detested the custodian's habit of barking orders at him. His response manifested itself in the form of a party piece when defending corner kicks. As the opposition swung the ball into the box T.G. would head it back for a vexed Sagar to catch. T.G. commented: 'Being a tall fellow he [Ted] invariably got the ball in the air, but if his path to it was blocked, I would shout to him and nod it back on the goal-line. The crowd may have gasped but I can assure you, we knew what we were doing.'[EP]

In contrast to T.G.'s recollections, Sagar's wife, Dolly, told the journalist Martin O'Boyle in 2001 that T.G. and Sagar were close: 'I think of all the players he played with, T.G. was Ted's favourite. They had an understanding between each other and they worked really well together. The pair of them used to talk for hours before the match about players who they thought could give them problems – and they continued their natter on the park.'

Whatever the exact nature of T.G.'s relationship with his teammate, the heading routine became synonymous with the pair over the twelve years in which they played together. Sagar would recall that it did not always go to plan: 'We did come unstuck once and the ball whistled past me from six yards' range.'[EP] One can easily imagine the air turning royal blue as Sagar went to retrieve the ball from the net.

Lining up alongside T.G. in the half-back line for the majority of the championship season were Joe Mercer and Jock Thomson. Thomson, the battle-hardened veteran of the 1932 league title win, had reclaimed his place in the team at the expense of Cliff Britton, with Mercer switching to right-half. Although Britton was an artist, almost unrivalled in his ball distribution abilities, T.G.'s preference was to play alongside wing-halves and full-backs who exuded physicality, giving him the time and space to orchestrate proceedings from the centre of the pitch. He reflected on this in 1970: 'The best wing-halves I played in between were Joe Mercer and Jock Thomson. For power, strength and ability I don't think there could be any better than those two. Mind you, Cliff Britton was a fine player, a brilliant player on the ball, but you had to get it for him. Mercer and Thomson could get it for themselves and do plenty with it.'[EP] Britton would continue to play with distinction in the second eleven, taking on some coaching duties to embark on a path which would lead him back to Goodison Park as manager a decade later. He would make one final league appearance in the spring of 1939, with the title effectively won.

Everton were to prove vulnerable as playing surfaces deteriorated with the onset of winter – compromising the team's swift passing game. Three losses in December, including one at Derby County, seemed to put the East Midlands club in the driving seat for the championship title, and 1939 got under way for the Merseysiders with a return to the Baseball Ground in the FA Cup. The squad had spent the preceding days recuperating and preparing for their forthcoming fixtures at a hotel in Harrogate. The methodical approach employed by Harry Cooke and Theo Kelly, as reported by Pilot, would not have been out of place in modern-day sport:

> *Everything in the Blues programme is arranged to the smallest detail. For instance, promptly at ten o'clock, four cars arrived at the hotel and the entire party (in addition to the players, Messrs Ernest Green (chairman), and George Evans, directors, Mr. Theo Kelly, secretary, Mr. Harry Cooke, trainer, and myself, were included) was whisked away to the icebound ground of the Harrogate club. The players wore special training boots – the invention of Harry Cooke – with short studs and were able to do their laps and sprints despite the conditions. Some then went out on the Wetherby road to complete their running and walking and on return found that the enterprising Harry Cooke had found some tennis*

courts which would enable the lads to have a six-a-side game.
The aim of the game is to acquire speed in passing. There is
no tackling. The players must part as soon as they are chal-
lenged. This means that the ball is continually on the move.
Players get the habit of quick passing – and in taking passes
sharply. (EP)

The respite and preparation paid off. Alex Stevenson returned from injury to
add his craft to the forward line, while learning from the defeat before Christmas,
Mercer and Thomson snuffed out the threat from Dix and Astley. The diminu-
tive Wally Boyes, of all people, got his head to a Bentham cross to put Derby out
of the cup with the match's only goal. This marked the beginning of an unbeaten
streak which would end, in the absence of Ted Sagar and Stan Bentham, with the
aberration of a 0–7 defeat to Major Buckley's Wolverhampton Wanderers. Nor-
mal service was resumed in the league with Sagar's return to the Everton ranks.

At 21 T.G. was still maturing as a player and match reports would highlight
shaky phases in matches, or the occasional slip. Tellingly, however, the reports
would almost invariably go on to describe how he recovered his confidence and
performance level quickly. When Everton drew with Birmingham at St Andrew's
in a cup tie it was noted: 'Jones was in great form. He once dribbled past three
men in the defence of his goal.'(FE) In the replay, won by Everton, T.G. was dish-
ing up more of the same: 'Jones, in the coolest calmest manner, beat two men in
the space of a sixpence... some were shouting to him to "Get shut" but Jones has
his own way of playing football.' (LE) The journalist Stork, in February, felt moved
to comment:

When Everton...are without Tommy Jones, that makes a big
difference to the side. Suppose Wolverhampton took Cullis out
of the half-back line – it would unbalance the team, or, at
least upset things. Jones's value to Everton is immense. He can
stop 'em equally as well as Herbie Roberts used to do, and has
that added charm and artistry. I hear a lot of talk as to the
best centre half-back playing in football. Well, my verdict goes
to Jones, even though I have a very high opinion of Cullis.(LE)

T.G. was given the honour of leading Wales on to the pitch for the first time on 15 March 1939. The match, a 3–1 victory over Ireland in the British Championship, was played at Wrexham's Racecourse Ground. In 2002, he told the Bangor and Anglesey Mail how it felt: 'One of the proudest moments of my career was being captain for Wales. I remember feeling that it couldn't get any better.' It was reported that T.G., brimming with pride at his elevation, forgot to bring his football boots to the match. A last-minute car dash to Connah's Quay, care of a good Samaritan, saw the footwear delivered to the ground in time for the kick-off. With play under way T.G. and goalkeeper George Poland excelled in keeping the opposition at bay according to match reports: 'Tom Jones held up the path to the Welsh goal, rarely giving Milligan and company room in which to operate.'[EE]

The sense of fun and camaraderie in the Everton camp that season was encapsulated in a vignette recounted by Pilot. It concerned when the squad stayed again at Harrogate in preparation for a crucial match against Sunderland in the title run-in:

> *Norman Greenhalgh purchased three mice in Harrogate and carried them everywhere. His demeanour after that win at Sunderland was typical of the unruffled manner in which Everton are marching to their triumph. Norman left the mice in the dressing room, and as he came back after the victory, his first words were: 'I must go and see if the mice are all right.' Norman has now given the mice to Tommy Jones, who believes they are good mascots. 'We haven't lost since we got them,' said Tom. 'No,' interposed Tommy Lawton, 'and we won a few matches before we got them.'[EE]*

What fate eventually befell T.G.'s mice was not recorded for posterity. The championship was effectively won over the Easter weekend in early April. Having defeated Sunderland at Roker Park on Good Friday, Everton travelled directly by train to London and defeated Chelsea the next day. Sunday saw the players report to Goodison for massages and light training before Sunderland were hammered there 6–2 on Easter Monday. Perhaps because of complacency creeping in, the coronation was delayed by the two subsequent matches being drawn and lost. In the end it didn't matter, as Wolves' failure to win at Bolton secured the title. The home season was rounded off with a comfortable victory over Aston Villa before a relaxed team lost to Grimsby at Blundell Park on the final day of the season.

The players' reward from the club's hierarchy for the championship success was modest, as T.G. recalled ruefully: 'Do you know what Everton gave us as a present? A half-day trip to Morecambe! You could take your wife or girlfriend if you so wished. I didn't go anyway; I didn't think it was worth travelling from Connah's Quay to Liverpool to travel to Morecambe for half a day.'[RT]

Everton had seemed set fair for a league and cup double in the 1938/39 season, but came unstuck in a Molineux morass. The cup tie against Wolves was given added spice by Tommy Lawton's insinuation, after Everton's heavy league defeat to their hosts, that the glazed look in the eyes of some opponents was due to them being 'doped up to the eyes' with monkey-gland extracts. (That some Wolves players were being injected with the extract was common knowledge at the time, but whether it had the effect Lawton alleged is less certain.) Everton prepared diligently at their training camp in Harrogate with revenge in mind. However, their brisk, swift, passing football approach would be nullified by tactics that were not exactly within the spirit of the game. T.G. would recall how the Toffees' FA Cup dreams sank in the quarter-final quagmire: 'We were top, they were second, and it was the sixth round of the Cup. If we won, we were in the semi-final. When we walked out onto the pitch we couldn't believe what we saw. They'd had the ground flooded all week... and the water had only been let off on the morning of the match. It was up to your ankles in mud. They beat us two-nothing. We never had a look-in. You spent as much time on your bottom as you did on your feet.'[RT] The episode would lead to Everton petitioning the Football Association to ban the excessive watering of pitches.

What is remarkable, in the context of modern football, is that out of 462 individual Everton league appearances during the course of the season, 436 were made by just twelve men. Norman Greenhalgh was the sole ever-present, but the likes of Joe Mercer, Ted Sagar, Torry Gillick, Billy Cook and Wally Boyes each missed only one or two matches. Senior club professionals such as Charlie Gee, Cliff Britton, Jimmy Cunliffe and Robert 'Bunny' Bell remained in the squad but were only called upon sporadically, when injuries necessitated.

Although Tommy Lawton, who hit 38 goals (34 league, 4 FA Cup), Mercer,

Gillick and T.G. were the stars of the side, the title success was built on the chemistry and cohesiveness of the whole squad – both on and off the pitch. Stork, writing in the Echo, highlighted an ethos of shared responsibility on the pitch and harmony off it: 'Unanimity of purpose has done the trick which only goes to show what can be done when there is happiness among the lads; what can be done when a team is composed of players who put team spirit before anything else. Individuality has a part in football but it is team spirit which pulls off championships.' T.G. would highlight the unheralded contribution made by the man he referred to as 'the engine room': 'Stan Bentham wasn't a good footballer but he'd run forever. He did the donkey work for everybody – he could run all day long. Some of the good players didn't like to run a lot but Stan did it all for them.'[JR]

Ranger was thrilled at the surprise upturn in the club's fortunes and could not resist a side-swipe at rivals Wolves in his Liverpool Echo column:

> At the beginning of the season I wouldn't have given tuppence for Everton's championship prospects. That, however, doesn't detract from my pleasure and sincerity in saying 'Well done.' They have succeeded by sound, skilful football and polished artistry – without glands or doctored grounds – on sheer merit; based upon a true scientific exposition of the game, as opposed to the modern craze of speed, hard-hitting, and first time tactics.

T.G. reflected in 1990: 'That was a truly great side. We never seemed to have to run about. We just pushed the ball to each other and everything went like clockwork. It is a great pity that the war broke out because I am sure we would have gone on to great things.'[EP] He expanded on this in conversation with Rogan Taylor: 'We were a great side. They called us "The School of Science". Believe me when I tell you, there were games when I went on the field and didn't break sweat – it was that good.'[RT]

What followed should have been a period in which 'The School of Science' entered a trophy-laden era. What actually transpired was summed up nicely by Norman Greenhalgh: 'What happened? Bloody Adolf Hitler, didn't he?'[RT]

THE WAR YEARS

IN THE SUMMER OF 1939, THE VICTORIOUS EVERTON SQUAD
embarked on a post-season tour of Switzerland and Holland – Germany had
been removed from the itinerary in light of the darkening political situation
engulfing the Continent. In spite of Neville Chamberlain's dash to Munich in
September 1938, allegedly bringing about 'peace for our time', Nazi-led Germany continued to flex its muscles in pursuit of Lebensraum. In March 1939,
Britain and France had pledged to defend Poland should it encounter further
German aggression. Europe now held its breath.

Nonetheless, on Merseyside, Everton's preparations for the 1939/40 season
got under way with great confidence that the team assembled would garner
further honours. The squad reporting back for pre-season training was virtually
identical to the one which had lifted the league trophy. About to turn 22, with
75 Everton appearances to his name, T.G. was entering the peak years of his
career, the same being true for Joe Mercer, Tommy Lawton, Alex Stevenson,
Ted Sagar and others. There were concerns over club captain Jock Thomson and

vice-captain Billy Cook, after both were involved in a car accident in Yorkshire. Cook received multiple wounds to his head and neck while Thomson fractured his collarbone.

Club chairman Ernest Green addressed the assembled squad of 42 players as they started their first pre-season training session at Goodison Park:

> *We knew we were up against it last year, and felt we had to fight hard to establish ourselves and get on the map. I am glad to say we did it so well as to win the championship. I have only one fear to the coming season, and that is because, being champions, we may feel it is going to be easy... I hope it is going to be as good a season as the previous one, and I wish you all every success.*[LE]

The new season was prefaced by fundraising matches across the country in aid of the Jubilee Fund, which sought to raise £40,000 to support former professional footballers. With Billy Cook declared sufficiently recovered from his car accident to lead the team, Everton lined up at Anfield against their Merseyside rivals with the team that had secured the league title: Sagar, Cook, Greenhalgh, Mercer, Jones, Watson, Gillick, Bentham, Lawton, Stevenson, Boyes. Liverpool ran out 2–1 winners but Leslie Edwards, using the 'L.E.E.' by-line, compared T.G. favourably to Matt Busby in the opposing half-back line: 'I liked Busby's quiet and effective use of the ball, but on this occasion he had to take second place to Tom Jones, another stylist, whose command of the centre of the field, and with such assurance and confidence, makes him the best centre-half in the game. By comparison Busby looked almost clumsy.'[DP]

The league season kicked off on 26 August against Brentford. Lawton was on target for the hosts in a 1–1 draw – a game in which Ted Sagar made his 300th senior appearance for the Blues. Lawton goals would follow in the following fixtures at Villa Park and Ewood Park. On Friday 1 September Germany launched an offensive on Poland and, with a heavy heart, Prime Minister Neville Chamberlain broadcast to the nation on the Sunday that war was being declared.

In spite of the uncertainty as to what might happen next, T.G. and his teammates reported to Goodison Park for training as usual. Theo Kelly, the club's secretary-manager, told the press: 'We shall carry on until we receive official word. That, I expect, will arrive after today's meeting of the Football League Management Committee.'

That committee was headed by Everton's long-serving former chairman, Will Cuff, who stated: 'I am advising all clubs of the Football League to instruct their players to stand by for the time being. The Management Committee will meet as soon as possible, and will then issue a statement.' On 8 September, the FA announced that all football was suspended until further notice. Clubs were permitted, in the exceptional circumstances, to tear up the employment contracts they held with their players, who were then obliged to join the armed forces or seek employment elsewhere. Uniquely among clubs, Everton paid up their players' contracts.

The cessation of the football programme would be a sickening case of déjà vu for Everton, who had been reigning champions in 1915 when the First World War led to a four-year hiatus in the league competition. Harry Catterick, a reserve-team striker at the outbreak of the Second World War, recalled to author John Roberts: 'I think the team that won the 1939 championship would have gone on to win two or three more had it not been for the war. There were so many good players.'

Non-competitive football did recommence quickly in areas deemed to be safe from German bombing, and Everton played out a 2–1 defeat to Blackpool at Bloomfield Road on 16 September. Lawton – naturally – was on target for the Blues. With the war in its 'phoney' phase, matches were permitted on Merseyside from late September onwards. Everton played friendlies with Preston North End and Liverpool, but attendances, suffered with fewer than ten thousand spectators present.

Nevertheless T.G.'s form in a 4–0 rout of Liverpool was so outstanding that Pilot gushed:

> If ever I saw the perfect centre half-back display it was provided by Jones, of Everton. A number of people said to me after the match, 'Busby was the best player on the field.' I disagree, and hand the palm to Tom Jones. Everton's display was an epic. They had pace, skill, a cheeky confidence, a flair for doing the unexpected in seeking the open space, finishing

accuracy and a perfect defence.[EE]

By October the championship squad was beginning to be eroded by an exodus of players to other occupations. Billy Cook, Jock Thomson, Joe Mercer, Tommy Lawton, Alex Stevenson, Wally Boyes and Cliff Britton would all become physical training instructors (PTIs) with the armed forces, and were posted around the country. They were joined by Wirral-born Stan Cullis, who with Cliff Britton and Joe Mercer would form a strong wartime England half-back line.

Of the other squad members, Charlie Gee became a demolition worker with the Air Raid Precautions organisation before retraining as a teacher, Norman Greenhalgh enlisted with the Royal Navy but was subsequently employed by Liverpool Corporation, Gordon Watson worked in a shipyard, Stan Bentham became an aircraft fitter at Burtonwood, and Jimmy Caskie returned to Glasgow to work in the Clyde shipyards. The depth of Everton's squad meant that the club was always able to field reasonably strong teams, with up to ten of its registered players guesting for clubs with depleted squads. A keenly felt loss was that of mercurial right-winger Torry Gillick. In November he suffered severe burns to his arm when his garage caught fire. Without the prompt actions of his wife in extinguishing the flames, the incident would have proven fatal. Gillick was admitted to Walton Hospital and would not play football for five months. He would only make one further Everton appearance before returning to Glasgow and rejoining his former club, Rangers, as a guest. His departure brought the curtain down on the Everton career of one of the most talented wingers to wear the royal blue shirt.

While T.G.'s brothers, Jack and Ellis, enlisted with the Royal Navy, he had his sights set on joining the RAF. His application was initially rebuffed, however: 'I volunteered for the RAF when the war started. At first they wouldn't take me as I was more use to them building bombers than joining up. They told us that the war wouldn't last more than six months so they got us jobs. They got me one at Broughton, between Hawarden and Chester, making Wellington bombers. I stayed there for six months. I kept playing for Everton as much as I could – or for anybody else. You could go and play on a Saturday and that was the end of it – there were no contracts. If you were a very good player you got a fiver, most players played for pretty near nothing.'[JR]

A regional wartime league was devised in October 1939, the aim being to minimise travel for teams and supporters. Everton would be pitted against traditional rivals such as the two Manchester clubs and also smaller ones like Chester, Tranmere Rovers and Stockport County. This campaign kicked off for Everton at Goodison on 21 October with a 4–4 draw with Stoke City. T.G. would get on the score-sheet with one of his trademark powerful free kicks, which Stork described: 'Jones' free-kick goal was a snorter, his namesake in the Stoke goal not having time to move before the ball was at the back of the net.'[LE]

T.G. would also make numerous representative appearances during the war, the first of which was in a Red Cross fundraising game at Goodison Park on 4 November. He scored a penalty for the All-British XI in a 3–3 draw against a Football League side featuring Tommy Lawton and Joe Mercer. A week later he put into his own (Welsh) net when facing England at Cardiff. The own-goal habit continued the following Saturday in a further defeat to England at Wrexham's Racecourse Ground. Watched by around 17,000 spectators, T.G. deflected a Lawton shot into his own net. One can only imagine the ribbing he received from Messrs Mercer and Lawton after the full-time whistle.

Own goals were an occupational hazard for a centre-half making last-ditch interceptions. These aside, T.G. was in the form of his life during the 1939/40 season. Sadly, his displays were wasted on meagre crowds and sometimes inferior opposition provided by lower (peacetime) league clubs. Each week Merseyside journalists struggled to come up with new superlatives to describe the immaculate performances. This selection of extracts from match reports written by Ranger, Pilot, Watcher, Contact and Bee in the autumn of 1939, reproduced below, gives a flavour of the high esteem in which T.G. was held:

Jones was the star in the Everton defence, as the Reds swarmed to the attack while making the mistake of holding the ball a trifle too long... Jones, incidentally, was as ever the kernel of the Everton defence.[EE]

Everton did not lose because the slight defensive failings in the side were more than counterbalanced by Tom Jones. Centrepiece of a half-back line which must be about the best in the country, he judged the right moment to step in and carve his way through the rather tame finishing of Liverpool's inside-forwards. (DP)

The dominant factor in the game was the Everton half-back line. Tom Jones was easily the best man on the field – the personality who consolidated the Blues' lines and yet played with extreme coolness. (EE)

Only Jones' rallying of the mixed forces at his disposal prevented the other side penetrating the defence. Jones is a Maginot in himself! The beauty of his play is its quiet effectiveness. He does not pull himself out of shape in desperate defensive stuff, but the impression one gets is that all opposing forwards dislike his nip-in-and-take-when-it-pleases-me attitude. With Watson and Lindley alongside it makes as all-round a half-back line as Everton ever had. (LE).

Jones was the essence of coolness, and his positional play was brilliant. He did no more than was absolutely necessary yet he completely dominated the Port Vale inside-forwards when the occasion arose. (EE)

The way Tommy Jones is going on he will be the season's top scorer, for his two goals against Blackburn Rovers in the Lancashire Cup-tie at Ewood Park brought his total of goals for the season up to seven. Some have been 'for' and some against, but his latest two were grand goals. Jones was invincible. The more I see of him, the more I consider he is the best centre half-back of any time. He was so confident, so correct and so dominating that he seemed capable of playing the whole of the Rovers team. (LE)

National fame and hero status on Deeside did not place T.G. above the law.

Having purchased his first car in the spring of 1939, he fell foul of wartime black-out regulations the following December:

NOTED WELSH FOOTBALLER FINED

Thomas George Jones, the Welsh international and Everton footballer, whose address was given as Pen Y Llan Street, Connah's Quay, was fined 10s at Northop Police Court to-day, for not having the front lamp of his motor-car screened with a regulation mask. Police Constable Jones said that when he examined the lamps on the evening of December 3 he found that they were covered with a thick cloth with holes cut in the centres. The reflector was not darkened, while the bumpers and running-boards were not painted white. Jones was alleged to have told the constable that he had painted the bumpers and running boards white on the previous day, and the rain had washed off the paint. Jones did not appear, but in a letter expressed regret for the offence, and stated that he was under the impression that his light conformed to law. (EE)

Motoring offences aside, on the pitch T.G. was moved up front as Everton pressed for a winner against Liverpool in one of two Christmas derby matches, scoring a penalty in the process. This would be the first of a number of occasions during wartime in which he was pressed into a more advanced position. As 1939 came to a close, Pilot reviewed the events of the previous twelve months and contemplated T.G.'s progression:

During last season the discussion arose as to the three best centre-halfbacks in football. I placed them in this order; Atkinson (Bolton Wanderers), Tom Jones (Everton), and Cullis (Wolverhampton Wanderers). This order needs revision. Without any fear of contradiction, Tommy Jones now stands out as the king of them all. His form this season is sensational. The remarkable thing is that he is so highly effective and yet so cool. He seems to amble through a game and yet in the air, or on the ground, is almost an impassable barrier. Tommy is coming to the front as a goal scorer, too. He has taken over Willie Cook's job as penalty taker, and has yet to fail with a spot-kick. He is deadly with those penalty line free-kicks. As Jones is playing at the moment I doubt whether there has ever been a better centre-half – and I am not forgetting those such as Frank Barson. (EE)

Perhaps these rave reviews went to T.G.'s head. In the first match of 1940, and desperate to atone for a missed penalty against Blackpool, he was reported to have neglected his defensive duties 'to go out on an attacking mission'(DP). The Seasiders, benefitting from the defensive gaps, ran out 2–3 winners. Perhaps focusing on himself rather than the team was an indication of the later egotistical streak which some would accuse T.G. of possessing towards the conclusion of his Everton career.

In mid-January, T.G. made his first return with Everton to Wrexham FC for a club fixture that was the first ever competitive match between the two sides. Hopes that another great centre-half, Stan Cullis, would guest for Wrexham were dashed when he was called up for an Army match at Crystal Palace. Stork wrote:

I am sorry Cullis will not be in the Wrexham team, for it would have been a fine sight for the Welshmen to see Tommy Jones, their own boy, and Cullis in opposition. I have no doubts whom they would plump for, and it would not be Cullis. Jones made his name with Wrexham, and Wrexham does not forget it. His name compares more than favourably with those of Fred Keenor and Tommy Griffiths. (LE)

T.G.'s performance did not disappoint his Welsh admirers. Pilot, reporting on the game, noted:

It must have been a little ironical to the 1,950 Wrexham supporters who paid £88 to see one of their former players so persistently holding up their own attack. This was Tommy Jones, whom Everton secured from Wrexham for a moderate fee and who now ranks as the best centre half-back in the game. Jones was the centre piece of a brilliant Everton defence which outshone the attack. Rarely have I seen the Everton forwards so ineffective. (EE)

In February 1940, Ranger once more extolled T.G.'s virtues:

One of the outstanding features of T.G.'s play, to my mind, is that he is seldom out of position. His anticipation puts him always in the right spot at the right time, and so sound is his judgement that now and again there seems to be something uncanny about it. I asked the Welsh international about it once. He confessed that he couldn't explain it, beyond his anticipation it was not the result of any conscious working out of a probable position. Though Jones himself may not be conscious of any methodical working out of probabilities, it must be going on subconsciously in his mind, like a sum, with every move of the play, and intuitively the result of the sum is always there in front of him. That sort of thing is a valuable gift to a footballer. It is either there or it isn't, a kind of bounty from nature. Practice may help a player develop the facility to some extent, but only the men who have it naturally are, like Jones, invariably right. (EE)

T.G.'s scintillating form led to his being handed the Everton captaincy for the first time as the Blues crossed the Mersey to play Tranmere Rovers in the Liverpool Senior Cup semi-final on 2 March. Soon afterwards, after much nagging on T.G.'s part, the RAF acceded to his request to join up. He recalled: 'After a few months I got fed up with [working in the aircraft factory] and went to Chester to apply to join the Air Force. I kept trying and eventually they got fed up and said, "OK, all right," and they took me in.'(JR)

The call-up was delayed several times. On 22 March at Maine Road, T.G. suffered the first significant injury of his football career and was carried off the field of play with an ankle injury. A fracture was feared at first, but subsequent diagnosis confirmed a severe sprain. With T.G. rushed back within three weeks, the ankle suffered further damage, resulting in more rest. Finally, in June 1940,

T.G.'s RAF service commenced. He described it thus: 'I was a Sergeant Physical Trainer in the Air Force – keeping the lads fit. I was sent to Weston-super-Mare for my initial training. They sent me up to Scotland and I was all over the place. St Athan in South Wales was another and on the other side of Preston.

'As soon as they knew who I was, I was put in the RAF team. Most of them were Arsenal players – they were the team in those days. The RAF offered me a commission but I didn't want it. For what I wanted, sergeant was the best rank possible as you didn't need a pass to get away at weekends. So I was able to travel anywhere at weekends and play for the teams I wanted to – you could play for a different one every week.'[JR]

Over the course of the war, T.G. would guest for several clubs – namely Tranmere Rovers, Wrexham and Swansea Town – as his RAF postings took him around the country. Fortunately for Everton, much of his RAF service was based at Hawarden, just a few miles from his hometown. In addition to nine wartime international appearances, in which he was habitually the team captain, T.G. would play alongside the likes of Stanley Matthews, Raich Carter and Ron Burgess in an RAF XI: 'During the war I played for the crack RAF team with Stan Matthews and all that crowd. We used to entertain people up and down the country.'[AS]

September 1941 saw T.G.'s Everton take on a Bolton side spearheaded by sixteen-year-old Nat Lofthouse, a man dubbed 'Lawton the Second' in the press. Pilot noted: '"Watch Lofthouse", I was told. I did and early on saw him side-step Tommy Jones and with the coolness and skill of the master player, but Tommy Jones never gave him another chance and marshalled a cool, methodical defence so well... Lofthouse has the head, the foot and the build to make a good 'un.'[EE]

Over the course of the war, a small but dedicated band of staff and players kept Everton Football Club ticking over. Foremost was the Stakhanovite Theo Kelly. Much maligned by some for his role in the departure of star players, his love of the club and organisational capabilities were beyond question. Kelly, who had served in the Royal Navy in the First World War, juggled the demands of managing the team and administrative duties with employment described in the local press as 'business of national importance'. He even helped to organise fire watches at Goodison Park when bombing was a grave threat. The team trainer, Harry Cooke, continued an unbroken run of service to the club which stretched back to the first decade of the twentieth century. On the playing staff, Norman Greenhalgh, Stan Bentham, Alex Stevenson, George Jackson, Gordon Watson, George Burnett and T.G. clocked up more wartime appearances than any other players – due chiefly to their employment or military postings being in the region. T.G., who made 139 competitive wartime club appearances, would actively help Kelly source guest players when there was a risk of Everton not being able to field a strong eleven. In later life, he would bemoan his perceived lack of recognition for services rendered to the club in this period – perhaps overlooking the fact that many men of his age had been on the front line in theatres of war.

In September 1941, T.G. had the honour of serving as best man when Joe Mercer married Norah Dyson on the Wirral. Both men were clad in their service uniforms, also present was Theo Kelly.

For considerable periods of the 1942/43 season, T.G. was stationed in Scotland and South Wales. He wrote to Pilot in early February 1943 about a reunion meeting with his former club captain:

> *Tommy Jones is, at present, on a 'special' RAF course, but getting his football with Swansea Town, for whom he scored two goals last Saturday – both headers from corner kicks. Tom says that when in Scotland they had a game with Carnoustie and on the same side was Jock Thomson. 'It was good to have [a] chat with Jock,' writes Tommy. 'Jock's the same as ever and sends his best wishes to all Merseyside friends. At the game I met Billy "Golden" Miller, the former Everton forward. Last Saturday's result at Goodison Park came as [a] real shock to me. Whatever happened? Here's hoping they stage a recovery. Give my very best wishes to everybody.* [EE)

In September 1942, Tom was not released by the RAF to play against Manchester United at Maine Road (standing in for the bomb-damaged Old Trafford), so Everton gave a debut to another Welshman. Llandudno-raised Jack Humphreys had written to Everton asking for a trial and impressed sufficiently to be offered amateur terms. The centre-half was serving in the army at the time of his call-up to the first team. Although it was hard to conceive then, Humphreys would become T.G.'s rival for the Everton centre-half shirt in the post-war years and also receive an international cap. Humphreys' stepson, Gerry, who himself played for Everton in the 1960s, recalls the contrast between the two men: 'They were two different types of footballer. Jack was what you might call an old-fashioned centre-half. That is not to say that he couldn't play but he was a strong "stopper" type whereas T.G. was a footballing centre-half.'

Devastating news reached T.G. at the end of 1942. His brother Jack, serving as an able seaman for the Royal Navy, was declared missing in action. It would be early 1943 before it was confirmed that he had died on 20 November when his Atlantic convoy ship was hit by a German torpedo. Jack was the sibling with whom T.G. had the closest bond and the bereavement affected him deeply; decades later, T.G. would often talk about Jack to family members. Jack's name is inscribed on the naval war memorial in Plymouth. T.G.'s other brother, Ellis, had better fortune; serving on the troop ship HMS Brigadier, he survived the war at sea and went on to work as a plasterer in peacetime.

Posted back to RAF Broughton, close to home, T.G. was able to make more regular appearances for Everton in the 1943/44 season than he had in the previous one. He captained the side in the absence of Jock Thomson and Billy Cook, both of whom had effectively retired from playing. He had met the wonderfully named Cuthbert Tatters, an amateur winger for Spennymoor United and Durham posted to Broughton while serving as a corporal in the RAF Medical Corps. On New Year's Day 1944, T.G. brought Tatters to Goodison to play in a League War Cup (North) fixture against Chester. The winger made an instant impression on Pilot, who commented on the new boy 'quickly distinguishing himself by his speed, dribbling and canny positioning'.[DP] He was invited back several weeks later to appear in a Merseyside derby – this time at inside-left. Early in the first half, Tatters suffered a severe ankle injury. He twice left the field for treatment before returning as a virtual bystander on the wing. Such bravery contributed to a 4–1 victory but a subsequent X-ray revealed that the ankle was broken. Tatters would never play football at such a high level again (after the war, he migrated to Australia, where, known as 'Rags', he played an active role in the game as a player and coach). T.G.'s own performance was crucial to the success over Everton's arch-rivals. Ranger gushed:

The outstanding performance on the winners' side came

from Tommy Jones whom I still reckon the finest centre-half of modern times. Everything he did had the hallmark of consummate artistry. Jones visualises the game moves ahead of anybody else which is why he's always in the right spot at the right time, and can play his game in that nonchalant half-speed fashion which takes so little out of him. He is always as fresh at the end as the beginning. (LE)

T.G. felt some responsibility for seeing Tatters, the man he'd introduced to Everton, suffering a career-threatening injury. Little could he foresee that a similar fate awaited him. In April 1944, the Mersey giants locked horns again – this time in an epic two-legged quarter-final of the Lancashire Senior Cup. With the aggregate score ending even, a replay was arranged after considerable wrangling with the authorities (the Home Office was loath to permit the staging of midweek fixtures). Everton got off to an ideal start as T.G. came forward to head home a corner kick, but just four minutes later a last-ditch, goal-preventing tackle on Cyril Done damaged T.G.'s ankle. Unable to stand, he was chaired off the pitch. Done was mortified to have been involved in the injury: 'He came down, fell awkwardly and hurt his ankle very badly. A lot of people seemed to think that I had injured him. I was very upset at the very idea that I could be considered as injuring the great T.G. Jones.'(RT)

What happened next would sow the seeds of mistrust and discontent which would culminate in T.G.'s exit from Everton six years later. Sat in the dressing room, watching his ankle balloon, T.G. was approached by an unnamed Everton director and a member of the coaching staff. In spite of the obvious severity of the injury, the director, who was never named, tried to coerce him into returning to the action – much as had happened with Tatters weeks previously. When T.G. refused, he was left to make his own way back to his RAF unit in North Wales to receive treatment. T.G.'s resentment of the Everton official who tried to force him back on the field would simmer for decades. Remarkably, at the time, the dressing room incident was not reported in the press. The ankle injury was so serious that it would dog him for the rest of his life, eventually becoming arthritic. Although he would continue to play football for another fifteen years, the ailment hampered T.G.'s on-field performances, as Joe Mercer noted in a

1962 article. 'Before he hurt his ankle, which became chronic in the end... he was the hardest spot-kicker of a ball since Eric Houghton. Some of the goals I have seen him score from free-kicks from up to 30 yards had to be seen to be believed.'[WM]

T.G. was eventually referred to Everton's retained specialist, Mr McMurray, but elected to rest the ankle rather than take the considerable risk of going under the surgeon's knife. It would be the autumn of 1944 before he was able to play any kind of football. Having eased himself back in through some games with his RAF unit, he returned for Everton at the end of October. Theo Kelly elected to play him at left-wing and inside-forward, where the chances of suffering further ankle damage were less. His first appearance back for the Toffees was at Anfield, the scene of his injury.

By December, newspapers were reporting that T.G. was becoming frustrated with his lack of opportunities at centre-half. He told Pilot that he needed a run of games in his favoured role: 'Jones was unfit to take over half-back duties, but told me a couple of days ago that he felt certain that by continually playing, and giving the ankle a chance to strengthen and give himself the necessary confidence, he can get right back to peak conditions. In other words, Tommy said, "Give me a game there and I'll soon be all right."' [EE]

This frustration at being played out of position while on the comeback trail was despite T.G. often revelling in a more advanced role. Years later, he would pontificate to David France that he was as much a forward as a back, demonstrating the same versatility that fellow Welsh great John Charles would become renowned for in the 1950s. Playing at inside-forward alongside Tommy Lawton, T.G. notched hat-tricks twice within the space of a week in heavy defeats of Stockport and Tranmere.

Finally, in January 1945, T.G.'s ankle was deemed strong enough for it to withstand the rigours of the centre-half role when he reverted to that position for the final stages of a match against Bolton Wanderers. The cameo was enough for Pilot to salivate: 'He gave us 15 minutes of sheer delight in pivotal mastery and artistry.'[EE] Several weeks later, T.G. made it clear to Ranger that he was, in fact, still some way short of a full recovery: 'Tommy Jones tells me he is getting more confident each week about his ankle, and that the regular games he is now getting are just what he needed. All the same, he still has to go a trifle gingerly, and still needs twice-weekly treatment.'[LE]

On 9 July 1945, attired in his RAF uniform, T.G. married Joyce Gwendoline Thomas at St Mark's church in Connah's Quay. His best man was Harold Cock-roft, who had just returned home from a German Stalag. Joyce hailed from Shotton, close to Connah's Quay, and her father was a worker at the local steel plant. The newlyweds would honeymoon on the Isle of Man, where Joyce had relatives. They would return to holiday there on several occasions, sometimes with friends Joe and Norah Mercer. The family home was Windsor House on the corner of Pen Y Llan Street and Church Street, just a few doors down from his parents' house at number 25. The marriage would endure until death, nearly sixty years later, but it would not be without its strains. T.G., handsome, athletic and famous, was never short of female attention. A sometimes liberal approach to his marriage vows would lead to difficulties in both T.G.'s personal and professional life over the decades, and it seems that Joyce displayed remarkable forbearance to keep the marriage intact.

As the last of the wartime league seasons (1945/46) got under way, T.G. con-tinued to be troubled by his weakened right ankle. He would only manage to make ten appearances throughout the season, while his compatriot Jack Hum-phreys consolidated his position in the number 5 shirt. By this time, cracks were appearing in the squad as Tommy Lawton agitated for a transfer. Trapped in an unhappy marriage, Lawton was desperate to leave Merseyside and make a fresh start in London. A first transfer request was submitted in May 1945. The board, initially bullish about retaining the talismanic centre-forward's services, eventu-ally bowed to the inevitable and accepted an offer of £11,500 from Chelsea in November 1945. The departure left T.G. feeling bereft of a friend and a player who he respected greatly. Chelsea did enquire about taking T.G. to Stamford Bridge with Lawton but, after some deliberation, Everton's board rejected the approach for the Welshman. Surprisingly, an offer from Preston the following spring was tentatively accepted only for the board to reconsider and retain the centre-half. Why the board would consider selling another star player so soon af-ter Lawton could be explained by doubts as to the long-term prognosis on T.G.'s ankle and early indications that he was becoming disillusioned at Goodison.

When Everton travelled to Sunderland's Roker Park for a League North fixture on 27 October, the trip was covered in-depth by Picture Post. With the soon-to-depart Lawton playing in a Services match in Leamington, and Joe Mercer away on army duty, the article hinted at T.G. cutting himself off from colleagues in the absence of his two closest friends:

> *We had to travel on Friday before the match. Round about four o'clock we left Goodison Park for Lime Street Station where we were to meet those of the players who were going to travel with us all the way. One by one they began to arrive and reported to 'the chief' as they call Theo Kelly... As soon as he had shepherded his flock onto the train the energetic secretary organised a Solo [card] school which was still calling 'abundance' when we were drawing into Newcastle seven and a half hours later. At Manchester we were joined by two more members of the team, Rawlings and Boyes, the wingers... Rawlings farms his own land near Warrington, Boyes is in the Army.*

> *From time to time, from the far corner of the compartment, a blood-curdling roar could be heard... it was Norman Greenhalgh, the left-back and captain of the team, being mirthful. Later in the journey he burst into song... In contrast to the Solo school was a perfect study in relaxation provided by the six-foot-two centre-half Tommy Jones, still in Air Force blue, who read the whole evening and was apparently oblivious of his noisier neighbours.*

5

BIRTH OF THE NOMADS

T.G. WAS DEMOBBED FROM THE RAF IN APRIL 1946. ON HIS release papers his wing commander noted that T.G. was 'an efficient and capable NCO who has a strong sense of duty and responsibility'. In wartime the physical training section of the RAF was headquartered at Lancaster Gate, home of the Football Association. Given overall responsibility for training PTIs both at home and abroad was Wing Commander Walter Winterbottom. In 1946 Winterbottom was appointed as the FA's director of coaching and was subsequently given responsibility for the national team. His vision was for every club and school to have a certified football coach.

Looking back with his friend Orig Williams, for a newspaper article in the 1990s, T.G. was dismissive of Winterbottom and his coaching strategy. He labelled him 'an amateur' who had never played the game at the top level and suggested that Winterbottom had gleaned his knowledge from the likes of T.G., Stan Cullis and Joe Mercer during the war years. T.G. was being somewhat loose with the facts; Winterbottom had represented Manchester United as an amateur in the pre-war years before a chronic back condition ended his playing days.

What riled T.G. about Winterbottom's plan was that it saw teachers, rather than current and former professional footballers, delivering the training to youngsters: 'He got this top job with the Football Association and he wrote the manual… the professionals were gradually pushed out and schoolmasters were coming into the system. It was considered better for the schoolmasters to do it, but these fellows couldn't play football.'[RT]

T.G. attended an FA qualifying course at Birmingham in 1946, and the following year completed the FA Chief Coaches Course in Leeds. In spite of his Welsh nationality, and his scepticism about the FA scheme, T.G. was often seen wearing a shirt with the FA's three lions symbol emblazoned on the breast pocket. The Football Association of Wales, inspired by Winterbottom's blueprint, enlisted T.G. to hold coaching courses in Aberystwyth. The students were almost invariably teachers, and according to T.G., many were more interested in getting the certificate, blazer badge and pay rise than passing on footballing expertise to children. 'Good God, they thought they were gods,' was his disparaging comment to Orig Williams.

Later, T.G. would recall how his coaching role developed: 'Not long after the war I was chief coach to the Liverpool County FA, which was the largest FA coaching scheme in Britain, and I was a staff coach for the Football Association. We used to go round schools. I had lots of professionals from different clubs working for me, and I used to delegate where they should go. A great example I can give you now is Willie "Billy" Cook. He was a marvellous man for football. Despite being a full-back his control was immaculate, and I remember watching Willie, in Wallasey, at a school there. He watched them play for a little while and one boy went to trap it and missed it by a mile. Willie blew the whistle, got them all in a circle round him, and said, "Look, you all saw that, didn't you? Now watch this." He kicked the ball and it nearly went out of sight, up in the air, and it came down, and it was dead. "Did you see that?" They all saw it and they could all then practise and do it. Now, you could tell those boys from now till doomsday how to do it, and it would go straight in one ear and out the other; but Willie showed them how to do it – that is coaching. Today it is all talk and theory.'[RT]

There is no doubting T.G.'s desire to share his love of the game with youngsters; in his County FA role he would visit many schools, giving inspiring talks about the game. In November 1945, he approached Theo Kelly with a request to be permitted to become a general sports master at the Leas School in Hoylake. The request was agreed to on condition that it did not interfere with Everton's call on his services. It appears that, ultimately, T.G. did not take up the post, but he became closely involved with coaching in his own town.

During the war, Connah's Quay Scout pack played football against Shotton Boys Brigade on a regular basis. Jacky Coppack and Tommy Lumborg were always captains of the opposing sides. Although sporting rivals, a number of the boys were friends and they came up with the idea of amalgamating their teams. The scoutmaster encouraged Coppack and Lumborg to approach T.G., who was stationed at RAF Hawarden awaiting demobilisation. Answering the teenagers' knock on his door would set in motion the creation of a legacy that is tangible in Connah's Quay to this day. Nearly sixty years later, T.G. told the Daily Post's Tony Coates what happened: 'I was on leave from the RAF during the war and two lads, Jacky Coppack and Tommy Lumborg, came to see me in my house on the corner of Pen Y Llan Street. They asked me to help them form a junior team. I was a big name then and could pull a few strings.'

Another player, Richard Parry, was appointed secretary for the project and recalls how, with his interest piqued by Coppack and Lumborg, T.G. got involved: 'He came along to the Scout hut for the inaugural committee meeting of the club. T.G. was very helpful and he sort of took over in the formation of the team.' Bill Dudley, who was twenty at the time, recalls tactical talks T.G. gave to the teenagers as the club was being formed: 'When he first started, he got the lads together and used the pull-down green blinds in his parents' house to write down all the tactics.' Subsequently, T.G. negotiated the use of a room at the Halfway House pub for weekly soccer teach-ins. Richard Parry recalls: 'Youngsters from around the district came to join the club. T.G. organised the training; he introduced heading tennis and dribbling between a line of posts. He invited some of his friends to talk to us. These were Tommy Lawton, Joe Mercer and Ray Lambert of Liverpool. When kids are playing football they are like a swarm of bees after the ball so T.G. gave us lectures on strategy. He was teaching us positional play and the idea of calling out to pals when we wanted the ball. He taught us that when you are due to tackle an opponent you back off until you are backed up by teammates, so that if he gets past you he has to get past them as well. These were little tips that were new to us. He also told us how to use the pivotal, or third back, system as used so successfully by Arsenal.'

T.G. would recall these sessions to Tony Coates: 'The interest was tremendous. The boys were rubbing shoulders with household names and the side turned out to be better than we dared hope.'[DP]

Having 'liberated' essential football equipment from the RAF, his challenge was to locate a suitable ground for the team. A playing field, offered by the local council, at Custom House Lane School proved too small, so T.G. pledged to help. He knew of a football pitch where the defunct Connah's Quay Athletic FC had played. The land, next to the Halfway House pub, was owned by the Chester Northgate Brewery. T.G. recalled to Tony Coates how he negotiated for its use: 'I'm not ashamed to admit that, once again, I used my soccer standing to get the field for five pounds annual rent from the brewery.'[DP]

According to Richard Parry, preparing the notoriously sloping pitch for use was itself a team effort: 'We now had to get the ground ready as it was completely covered with two-foot-high grass. Tom's brother, Ellis, who was on leave from the Navy, scythed down the grass ready for a mower. I helped by stacking the grass. There was a disused building alongside the new pub and we were given use of that as a changing room.'

With the club suitably equipped, membership of the Northop and District Junior League was sought, as Richard Parry recalls: 'My next job was to send in an entry to the league. We were called to a league meeting in a pub in Northop, which is three or four miles away, so Tom and I cycled there. The people who were running the league were having drinks so Tom bought me some lemonade as I was too young to have alcohol.' With the application to join accepted, T.G. was also co-opted onto the league's executive committee.

Parry also recalls acts of kindness by T.G. which typified his desire to help young players: 'I had an old pair of football boots that my dad had repaired but they were pretty shot. Tom noticed these and he said, "Come along to the RAF station – bring your old boots and I'll exchange them for a new pair." And he did – courtesy of the RAF! On a couple of occasions Tom took my friend and I to see matches at Goodison, and got us seats in the press box.'

The new club was christened Connah's Quay Juniors. T.G. joined the new committee, persuading his friend, and Wales teammate, Billy Hughes to become chairman. One of the team's first fixtures was a pre-season friendly arranged by T.G. against an Everton Colts side containing future star forward Dave Hickson. Success in the club's debut 1946/47 campaign was immediate. With some boys becoming over-age for the Junior League, the club expanded to field a team in the Flintshire League, which carried no age restriction. The Welsh Youth Cup was secured in March 1948 with the defeat of Cardiff at Aberystwyth. T.G. was not present due to playing commitments but was promptly notified of the result: 'I'd just come off the field after playing Manchester United and was called to the phone. It was Billy Hughes. All he said was, "We've beaten the buggers and Tommy Lumborg got the winning goal!"'

T.G. remained actively involved with the club until the early 1950s, occa-sionally arranging friendly fixtures with Everton youth teams and 'T.G. Jones XIs'. Soon after the club's formation, T.G. approached the Everton board with a proposal that Connah's Quay Juniors foster links to Everton as a nursery club. This was met with a lukewarm response, and a request, made at the same time, for the club to provide him with a house in Connah's Quay was declined.

Joining the Welsh League in 1952, the Juniors were renamed Connah's Quay Nomads. In subsequent years T.G. was kept updated about the club's affairs by former player Geoff Thelwell and friend Nigel Wright – who posted the local papers each week to his homes in Pwllheli and Bangor. T.G. last attended a Nomads match when they entertained Shrewsbury Town in a 1983/84 Welsh Cup tie. The Nomads are currently known as 'gap Connah's Quay' (for sponsor-ship reasons) and compete in the Welsh Premier League, qualifying to compete in the 2016/17 Europa League.

WANT-AWAY

HAVING SUFFERED A KNEE INJURY WHICH NECESSITATED sticks to aid walking, T.G. was unavailable for selection in January 1946 when Everton fell to Preston North End at the first hurdle in the FA Cup. He had recuperated by the spring and was pressed into a centre-forward position when injuries necessitated – Bee noting that he 'brought his height and innate skill to bear upon the centre-forward role'[DP] when he hit a brace against Chesterfield.

Around this time, young supporter David Peate witnessed an exchange between T.G. and teammate Wally Fielding, which hinted at fraying relationships with Theo Kelly: 'I still collected autographs in those days and it was after a game that I got that of T.G. He had not been playing that Saturday and he came hobbling out onto Goodison Road with a walking stick. He leaned awkwardly on his stick as he held my little book. As he was signing, Nobby Fielding passed by and said, "Hey, Tom, Kelly's on his way. Watch out he doesn't kick your stick away." T.G. just smiled as he handed my book back to me.

After a seven-year hiatus, the Football League programme recommenced in

September 1946. The fixture list replicated that of the aborted 1939/40 season. Although the fixtures may have been identical, the same could not be said for the Everton squad. The 1946/47 squad was a pale imitation of those title-winning purveyors of 'scientific' football. Thomson, Gee and Britton had retired, Cook and Cunliffe had moved to lower league outfits, while Boyes, Sagar, Stevenson and Greenhalgh were past their prime. Of the younger stars, Lawton had departed for London while Gillick and Caskie had returned to Scotland. Behind the scenes Theo Kelly remained secretary-manager, a post he was elevated to shortly before the outbreak of war, although tactics and training remained largely outside of his scope. The evergreen Harry Cooke continued as trainer with former captain Jock Thomson becoming coach.

In spite of captaining Everton for much of the war, T.G. was overlooked for the role when the Football League competition resumed. Norman Greenhalgh was given the honour instead; the snub must have hurt T.G. Now approaching his 29th birthday, T.G., who sported noticeably longer hair than pre-war, was an elder statesman of the team. He commented wryly to golf-partner Tony Ensor a few years later: 'I had a curious career. Before the war I was this up-and-coming talent signed from Wrexham, and when I came back after the war I was this grand veteran.'

One significant squad addition was the bandy-legged Wally 'Nobby' Fielding, who had been spotted by Everton director Jack Sharp while serving in the army. Fielding would give a dozen years of service to the Toffees, playing into his late thirties. After T.G.'s death, Fielding shared his memories of the centre-half in an Everton programme article:

> When I first went to Everton... [T.G.] helped me settle in. Not only was he a wonderful person but a wonderful player too. He was the best centre-half I have ever seen play. He was truly brilliant. He was so calm and confident when the pressure was on; he passed the ball well and he had a remarkable understanding with Ted Sagar. He was always very 'dapper' – clean and smart. We used to joke that if he hadn't made it as a footballer he would have been a film star. It was a pleasure to know him and a pleasure to play alongside him.

A Sports Spectator publication dedicated to Everton, produced on the eve of the season, contained pen pictures of the squad. Its poetic description of T.G. tallied with Fielding's observations about the Welshman's photogenic qualities:

> *Would make a film talk. Would make a football film a veritable triumph. Tall, dark and handsome, is the centre-forwards' heart break. Heads with delicious effrontery; has a fierce free-kick drive and a nodding acquaintance with corner kicks in a forward line lacking height.*

At the season's opener against Brentford, the unenviable task of filling the void left by Lawton's exit fell to Harry Catterick – his league debut arriving nine years after he joined the club as a part-time professional. With Ted Sagar still serving in the forces, the team lining up against Brentford at Goodison Park was: George Burnett, George Jackson, Norman Greenhalgh (captain), Joe Mercer, T.G. Jones, Gordon Watson, John McIlhatton, Eddie Wainwright, Harry Catterick, Wally Fielding, Wally Boyes.

An under-par team performance led to a shock 2–0 defeat to the Londoners, although Bee commented: 'Jones gave such glimpses of his vintage form which so impressed Welsh FA watchers.'[EE] An away victory at Villa Park in the second fixture gave cause for misplaced optimism, with T.G. and Joe Mercer appearing to be picking up where they had left off in 1939. Pilot wrote: 'Joe was the Mercer of the real vintage, and his display would have hit every headline had it not been overshadowed by the finest exhibition of centre-half play I have seen for many a day. This was from Tommy Jones, who already is certain of his place in the Welsh team.'[EE]

Sadly, Joe Mercer's relationship with the Everton board had reached a nadir. Having been embroiled in several club-versus-country rows and then been expected to play without appropriate investigation and treatment of a debilitating knee injury, the wing-half submitted a transfer request in early September. Unsurprisingly, it was declined by Theo Kelly and the board, but Mercer was not to be deterred. In a precursor to T.G.'s actions four years later, Mercer was prepared to turn away from football rather than remain at Everton. He played his last match for the club he adored on 2 November, prior to taking a break from football to run a grocery shop on the Wirral. A few weeks later, Everton bowed to the inevitable and sanctioned a move to Arsenal. Here Mercer would receive the medical treatment his knee required, allowing him to play on for a further five years, winning two league titles and a FA Cup winners' medal in the process.

Losing his close friend, T.G.'s thoughts turned to his own Goodison future. In seeking to replace Tommy Lawton, Everton had missed out to Liverpool on signing Newcastle's Albert Stubbins; he would score many of the goals that ensured the league trophy moved across Stanley Park to Anfield. Spurned by Stubbins, Everton turned to the hefty forward Ephraim 'Jock' Dodds. T.G. had found Dodds a formidable opponent during wartime games but, a creditable goal return for Everton notwithstanding, the Scot was not in the same class as Lawton. T.G. was, once again, struggling with the ankle injury picked up at Anfield in 1944. He could not sustain a run of games without breaking down again, but this did not stop him earning plaudits. When Southend were put to the sword 4–2 in a January 1947 FA Cup encounter, Ernest Edwards' report summed up T.G.'s approach, which had trodden a fine line between scintillating and cavalier:

Jones risked all and many feared delayed action might bring a goal against him at a most inconvenient moment. Against that hold-off, one has to put in the scales of justice the numberless times Jones trapped the ball with consummate art, and also his nonchalant passing to an unmarked comrade, and a run in which he took the ball through as though it were tied to his boot. Jones caught a strong challenge en route from three men, plus a testy charge, yet he carried on with his mission, undaunted and unbeaten. This was the outstanding run of the match – a streak of genius which came upon the dull world to the moment sunshine streaked through to light this unusual cup game. Jones not only did his pivotal work; he sauntered up to engage with corner kicks and no one can overestimate the value of his appearance in Southend's goalmouth when he took the first goal (three registered in two minutes) by a foot, not a header.

T.G.'s ankle problems recurred after this match, and with Theo Kelly and the directors' playing sub-committee understandably unwilling to risk him at less than 100 per cent fitness, Jack Humphreys enjoyed his first prolonged spell in the number 5 shirt since peacetime. T.G., deprived of game time in a team rooted in mid-table, reached the conclusion that he needed to move on from Everton.

As the team travelled back by train from a friendly fixture at Millwall on Saturday, 1 March 1947, T.G. notified the directors of his desire to leave. The story broke in the Merseyside press on the following Monday morning. Soon supporters were writing in to local newspapers venting their frustration at the state of affairs. A typical letter, published in the Liverpool Echo, read:

> *The loss of Lawton and Mercer was serious but the contemplated loss of Jones is well-nigh unbearable. Popular gossip attributes these requests to many causes and it is a noticeable fact that internationals in their prime never used to leave the Everton Club. One also remembers famous players who have refused to join them this season, from Stubbins, downwards. There must be a reason for all this. Should the Jones transfer come to be, I think a general boycott should be the order of the day.*

Looking back, T.G. revealed that he had been 'tapped up' by other clubs to leave Everton, but securing a transfer in the 1940s was not a straightforward task without the blessing of the club: 'The team went from the best to the worst – they brought players in who couldn't bloody play and Ted Sagar and I were keeping them in the league. I got fed up with this and applied for a move. Joe Mercer had been in touch for me to play for Arsenal – they wanted me. Matt Busby was at United and was [starting to] build a young side up. He got in touch with me and said, "Listen, Tom, I could do with you with all these young lads." So I asked to be put on the transfer list. I said to them, "You've let all your good players go and I want to go as well," but they wouldn't let me go. Apparently I was worth more to them than all the rest put together.'[JR]

Having had two transfer requests declined in the space of a fortnight, T.G. was briefly recalled to the first team in place of the injured Humphreys. However, in just his second comeback appearance he pulled a muscle as well as flicking the ball with his head past a furious Ted Sagar and into the Everton net. He would not appear in the senior side for the remainder of the season.

IN MAY 1947 A UNIQUE FOOTBALL MATCH WAS PLAYED AT
Hampden Park between Great Britain and a Rest of Europe side. The beneficiaries
were FIFA, after world football's governing body found itself near bankruptcy at
the end of the war. T.G. was struggling to shake off his muscle injury, probably
making him ineligible for selection for the match. The centre-half spot went to
Jackie Vernon of Second Division West Bromwich Albion. The Everton faithful
fulminated for weeks with indignation at the perceived snub to their hero. The official explanation offered was that Wales already had representatives in the side and
that Vernon was the Irish representative. Furthermore, T.G. was some way from
being match-fit. This did not go down well with Evertonians and there was much
talk of someone on the Everton board scuppering T.G.'s chances. If nothing else,
the episode illustrates the esteem in which T.G. was held by supporters and the
poisonous atmosphere which was developing between club, player and supporters.
Tom Gardner, who made his solitary first-team appearance for Everton in 1947,
spoke to me before his death in 2016. He recalled his impressions of T.G. and the
leniency afforded him by Harry Cooke in the post-war years: 'We called him "Big
Tommy". I think the reason was that there was also 'Young Tom' in T.E. Jones. As
a player, T.G. was one of the most perfect centre-halves that I have played with or
ever seen. He always seemed to be in the right place at the right time – a very hard
man to beat on the field – even in training. He appeared to be slow and I would
think, "He's never going to get there." But his positional play was unbelievable
and he was always there – a hard man to get past. His all-round performance was
absolutely superb.

'The trainer in those days was Harry Cooke. We used to train on Goodison
Park and a little bit at Bellefield. Harry was a bit of a stickler for time – if us young
fellas were five or ten minutes late he'd give us a dressing down, but T.G. travelled
from Wales and was always late! I don't think he ever turned up on time – he was
usually ten or fifteen minutes late. He used to come straight to the dressing room,
come out to the field and do his training more or less by himself – he had his own
routine. T.G. was his own man and seemed to do the things that he wanted to do
in training, and Harry let him get on with it, whereas we were forced to do what
Harry told us to do. He mixed with the lads but he was a quiet type. When I first

went to Everton I thought, "Oh God, I'm going to play with Tom Jones." But he was just like a gentleman – a really nice man.'

It seems likely that T.G.'s individual training regime, as described by Gardner, was driven both by his ongoing ankle complaint and his feeling of disenchantment at the club.

Being spoiled for choice in the centre-half position was a mixed blessing for the Everton directors as it proved near-impossible to keep both T.G. and Jack Humphreys happy. When Humphreys found himself out of favour with the selectors, he took a leaf out of T.G.'s book and submitted a transfer request. Humphreys was back in favour for the start of the 1947/48 season and his transfer request was put in abeyance.

Aware of renewed interest from Chelsea, who remained keen to reunite him with Tommy Lawton, T.G. had submitted a third transfer request. Weeks short of his thirtieth birthday, and increasingly disillusioned, he wrote to request an audience with the board at their meeting on 23 September. He recalled in 2000: 'I asked to see the board of directors. I went and met them at their meeting and said, "Now look, the position is this: I've been here long enough. Other clubs want me and I want to go." I was thirty then [sic]. You didn't play until forty; thirty was a good age then. But they wouldn't let me go even then.'[JR] The appeal to the directors actually coincided with a brief recall to the first team, but when dropped again, he lodged yet another transfer request. He was quoted candidly in the local press: 'It is a long and bitter story. While I would rather play for Everton than anybody, and in spite of all that has happened I still reckon them to be the best club in the world, the fact remains that latterly the position has become intolerable.'

Commenting on being dropped from the first team to face Middlesbrough, he added:

It is a cruel blow, and the public can judge for themselves whether I have been unworthy of my place in the first team. I think it most unsporting, even in [the] face of the Bolton defeat, to omit me the day after I had been chosen to represent Wales versus England. It is equivalent to saying to the Welsh FA, 'This man is a Central League player, and does not find favour with his club, which prefers his compatriot, Humphreys.[LE]

Theo Kelly's retort, given to Pilot, was succinct and emphatic: 'Jones came to me after the team to meet Middlesbrough had been issued and for the fifth time asked to be placed on the transfer list. I refused the request. Everton cannot afford to allow Jones to depart, and will not allow him to depart.'[LE]

Having failed to force a move to a top-flight rival by conventional means, T.G. took the almost unheard of step of enlisting the media's help in agitating for a move. He told the journalist Alan Hoby of his grievances dating back to 1944 and, it would appear, tacitly approved their publication in the People. Although T.G. was not named in the resulting piece, it was patently clear to readers that Hoby had been provided with first-hand source material:

26 OCTOBER 1947
HOBY ON SPORT
SOCCER STARS BULLIED BY DIRECTORS

One thing about football – you can't 'fix' a League game like you can some fights. Just the same, there is plenty that has a nasty smell even in soccer. Have you ever asked yourselves, for example, who are the directors of your local football club, or what qualifications – if any – they possess for the complex, highly specialised, job of running a modern professional side? If not, it's time that you did.

There are two types of director – the rare sort, with brains as well as a bank balance, and that ever growing horde of boardroom buffoons who don't know a footballer from a floor-walker. But the old-time 'boss' manager is a dying breed. Today we have this puerile, puny race of upstart directors in control of clubs... He refuses to recognise that the successful running of a football club is primarily the job of a paid team manager – preferably an intelligent ex-player who knows the technical side of soccer from every angle.

Take the case of a famous international footballer (you would know his name as well as those of your own wives) who, in a friend's words, is being hounded out of football. I bring this to your attention as this is the greatest player in the world in his position. Yet he can't command a place in his own first team although his country thinks him good enough to play for them!

Unfortunately for him, after scoring a brilliant goal, he badly damaged an ankle trying to stop the equaliser – he had to quit, he had no other choice – his ankle was swelling like a balloon. Yet, although he was in great pain and scarcely able to hobble, one of his directors – with a club official – followed him down to the dressing rooms and tried to order him to return to the field. The player refused – 'It would have ruined his career,' a friend said, 'besides, he was an ambulance case.' Yet, so nettled were the club officials over the incident that this footballer, who had given them splendid loyalty and service, was left to get back to his unit alone, as best he could.

The above section of the article was a very thinly veiled reference to T.G.'s injury in the Merseyside derby in 1944. The article then went further – outlining the situation T.G. found himself in at the club in 1947, and taking a swipe at the directors' treatment of Joe Mercer:

But this is not the end. Since then various stories have been cooked-up. 'He is temperamental', 'He is not a good club man', 'He only plays when he feels like it', and so on. One director has even been overheard to say that he wouldn't even play him in the third team. But his own country doesn't think he's a third-team player. They picked him for the national side the night before he was dropped by his own club!

This same club, incidentally, not so long ago, tried to play a very famous wing-half at outside-right the week after he had captained England! The international refused – point blank. Today this same half-back skippers one of the most famous sides in the country.

It's not only petty, it's utterly preposterous.

Unsurprisingly, Everton's directors were furious about this public airing of the club's dirty laundry. The matter was discussed at the board meeting three days after publication of the article. The minutes recorded: 'An article in a Sunday newspaper was considered but whilst it may be libellous, it was decided to take no immediate action.' Perhaps the directors were all too aware that any legal action would lead to further public disclosure of Goodison Park's private affairs.

Any pretence of anonymity in the Hoby article was removed when T.G. subsequently made a candid and heartfelt statement via Ranger:

> *When I joined Everton from Wrexham ten years ago I hoped it would be the only signing in my career. My greatest ambition was to finish my active days at Goodison Park. Today, I want nothing so much as to get away. I have asked for my release five times. Five times have the board said 'No', although less than two years ago, the then chairman (Mr W.C. Gibbins) said Everton would never attempt to retain a dissatisfied player. Evidently views have undergone a change in the boardroom; I wonder why?*

> *Could it be that, having lost Tommy Lawton and Joe Mercer when both might have been kept had different methods been adopted, they are frightened of public opinion if they let me go? Even now I should not be making this public statement had not certain things which have appeared in print forced my hand. When you have read this statement you may not be on my side, though I sincerely hope you will, for I have the utmost affection for all your sporting folk of Merseyside. You have always been kind to me, I am grateful for your support and for the hundreds of sympathetic letters I have received.*

> *Now for my reasons. They go back to the Liverpool game at Anfield on April 22, 1944, the third time we had met in ten days to settle a Lancashire Cup-tie. Early on I suffered an ankle injury, and had to be carried off the field. While in the dressing room doubled up with pain, an Everton director came down, looked at my back and swollen ankle, and re-*

sponded to my remark that I wouldn't be able to return to the field. 'That's nothing,' he said, 'I've seen plenty of fellows play when much worse than that.' He was most annoyed when I refused to go back. I couldn't have done so for a thousand pounds. In any case, my future livelihood was at stake.

Sitting there pondering, my mind recalled an incident on the same ground three months before, when Cuthbert Tatters, a promising RAF lad I had brought to Everton, also received a severe ankle injury. But there was this difference. Tatters did go back, played in great pain and when his ankle was X-rayed on return to his unit it was found to be broken! That finished Tatters' career in first-class football. It might have been my fate also. I was left to get away from Anfield as best I could. Nobody seemed to care whether, or how, I got back to my unit or whether I would be fit to play again. As it was, I was in hospital for four months and dared not touch a ball for six months.

After that, do you wonder why I'm sometimes cynical when Everton assure me how much they think of me? It was not until some weeks later when the RAF decided an inspection was necessary, that Everton interested themselves, and got their own specialist to do it. During the three weeks I was in hospital in Liverpool no official of the club came near me. Was this further evidence of my value to the club, I wondered? If so, it was a queer way of showing it.

During the time I was off injured, I was deposed from the captaincy. Tommy Lawton, still one of my greatest friends, was appointed in my place. I didn't mind that a bit. What did upset me was that I was not notified of the change. I first learned of it from the press while lying in hospital. Returning soon after the start of the following season, I had played about a dozen matches when my ankle went again, and Joe Mercer, another of my staunchest pals, had two or three games *as an emergency centre-half. You can guess my feelings when Joe informed me that a club official had said he would far rather have him at centre-half any day than me. Could this, I wondered, be yet another example of how much I was valued?*

When I was once more fit, Jack Humphreys was in the side and I was rarely chosen. During that time, and since, malicious tales have been circulated about me – some to the effect that I would only play when I felt like it, picking my matches when the opposition was easy. Others asserted I was not a good influence in the team, and made me out to be all that a bad player is supposed to be. And so it went on. Where do these harmful rumours originate? In the dressing room – or elsewhere? I have never been able to pin them down, but certainly they are not calculated to make me feel happier. Then six months ago, Mr W.C. Cuff publicly stated that a certain person connected with the club had said, in the hearing of many people, that 'Jones and Mercer are no good to any club'. So far as I am aware, that statement has never yet been denied. In any case, a man of Mr Cuff's standing would not have made such an accusation without proof.

From another source, I understand, a director has asserted that if he had his way he wouldn't play me in the first team. Yet another has stated that I only want to leave in order to make money out of my transfer. Is it any wonder that I feel the sooner I get away the better? How can I settle down in the face of that? I say nothing about being dropped this season after only two league games, I leave the public to form their own conclusions. Was I dropped on form or for what other reason? Suffice to say that Jack Humphreys, himself, confessed to me that he was astonished when he heard it. 'So what?', I thought, 'that is not the point.' If the board prefers Jack to me, I'm not grousing, I wish him all the luck in the world. But I am convinced that if Jack Humphreys wasn't taking my place it would be somebody else. I may be wrong, but it is my firm conviction, which the trend of events behind the scenes have done nothing to dispel, that I shall never get back to the Everton first team, except in case of dire emergency.

What I am kicking against are the malicious and untrue stories going about, the treatment I have had of recent years, as outlined above, and the discrepancy between that and the board's official attitude. Rightly or wrongly, I feel also that I am something of a scapegoat because I do not take part in certain special activities that do not appeal to me.

I could say much more, but already I've gone on at greater length than I intended. I am content to leave the matter with the public. Let me emphasise again however that I am anxious to get away from Goodison Park as soon as possible, I shall never settle down there again. If Everton still refuse my request, then I shall try to get a job outside football as soon as my current contract has expired. Whatever happens I shall honour that. But I do not want to leave football if it can be avoided. I am still a comparatively young player; without being boasting, I think I could look forward to several seasons in the senior side of any other First Division Club.(LE)

In fact, T.G.'s gamble in going public seemed to pay dividends when, at the subsequent board meeting, the minutes recorded that the directors had agreed: 'In light of all events, to notify certain clubs that we are prepared to consider his transfer.' The fee sought was in the region of £15,000 (or the equivalent value in player exchanges). When informed of the board's decision, while on international duty with Wales in Glasgow, T.G. told reporters: 'It would have been impossible for me to settle down again at Goodison Park. I feel it is best all-round that we should part company; I do not mind where I go. All I want is to get back to regular appearances in First Division football.'

Departing Goodison on far more amicable terms at this time was Jock Thomson, T.G.'s pre-war captain and teammate and Everton's post-war coach. The Scot took up the role of manager at Manchester City with the blessing of the Everton board.

A slew of clubs, Sheffield Wednesday, Notts County, Chelsea, Wolverhampton Wanderers, Derby County, Cardiff City and Bolton Wanderers included, contacted the Everton board to express interest in signing T.G. However, these enquiries appear to have been quietly rebuffed as offers failed to match the club's valuation of £15,000. T.G. recalled that the directors seemingly paid only lip service to the transfer-listing – hoping that he would rescind his request: 'Although they'd put me on the transfer list, they refused to let me go. I couldn't go anywhere. Arsenal told me that they approached the club and they [Everton's directors] said, "He wanted to be on the transfer list but he doesn't really want to go." Matt Busby was told the same. Whether they were afraid to let me go or not, I do not know.'[RT]

Joe Mercer was enjoying life at Highbury and it seems that he acted as an unofficial intermediary between T.G. and Arsenal. More than a decade later, Mercer would reflect on how the war and the drawn-out battle to leave Everton had tempered his friend's love of playing football: 'The war came at the very height of his career. Consequently, the football world never saw the best of T.G. because, somehow or other, he never seemed to regain the enthusiasm which made him such a great player in the pre-war era.' [WM]

Everton's board meetings in this period had 'T.G. Jones' as a standing agenda item. In December 1947, these records hint at T.G., in spite of his public pronouncements about moving, being conflicted in his wishes to leave the club at which he was adored by spectators. He would confess, fifty years later, 'I loved Everton, but they never loved me very much.'[RT] On one occasion, T.G. had proposed a compromise to the club chairman:

> *Dr. C.S. Baxter reported a tripartite conversation at Portsmouth when the player had inferred that he wished to stay with the Club if a guarantee could be given for his future after his playing days were over. The player needed such a guarantee even if transferred. It was felt that such guarantee was beyond our powers.*
>
> *Secretary is empowered to explain that his value to the Club was on the playing field at the present time.*

After this period of uncertainty, the board resolved, in Febru-
ary 1948, to retain T.G.'s services. It was agreed that this
player should be retained by us meantime.[BM]

While waiting in vain on transfer developments, T.G. was recalled to the first team in late November 1947 and impressed with his displays. Unfortunately, a further flare-up of his right-ankle condition occurred at Bloomfield Road on 3 January:

Jones may be on the injured list for a long time, for at Black-
pool on Saturday he injured the right ankle side (that wartime
injury which kept him inactive so long). The exact extent of
the damage is not known, but Tommy was under treatment
for nearly two hours at Goodison on Saturday night, after the
return from Blackpool, and Everton will not hesitate to place
Tommy under a specialist. Jones was having attention at the
touchline at Bloomfield Road when the first of Blackpool's
five winning goals went in. When, later in the dressing-room,
he heard the cheers greet the second goal he asked to go back
on the field just to fill a position. Secretary-manager Theo
Kelly, who was there, as ever zealously ruling the Everton
team, went to the dressing room with Jones and said to me
later: 'Tommy could hardly hobble and yet he would have
gone back on the field had I said yes.'

That typifies the spirit of our lads, just as the injury shows the
ill-luck you run against. Jones never has played better than
in the last few weeks, and now it may be weeks before he
plays again. Thank goodness we have such a grand lad as Jack
Humphreys to step in again. [EE]

T.G., when deemed fit again, would regain his place for the last eleven games of the season – another disappointing one in which Everton finished in four-teenth place in the league standings. Although the club had decided to retain T.G.'s league registration for the following season, T.G. was in no hurry to sign the contract papers. He informed Theo Kelly that he'd received the offer of a five-year contract, with a salary of £1,000 per annum, to be player-coach of an unnamed non-league club. A move to a club outside the jurisdiction of the four divisions of the Football League was attractive to T.G. as it would circumvent Everton's holding of his playing registration.

THIS MOVE AWAY FROM THE LEAGUE NEVER CAME TO

fruition but, with the squad in pre-season training for the 1948/49 season, sensational news broke in the Merseyside press. It was revealed that AS Roma were in negotiations to sign the Everton centre-half. In 1997, T.G. recalled to Paul Joyce how the potential switch was put to him: 'Theo Kelly called me up to his office and asked if I'd like to go to Italy. The war hadn't been over long and everywhere was in a hell of a mess, especially for the Italians. I thought about it and decided to have a go. Roma were the club interested and they were willing to match Everton's valuation.'[LE]

Roma had appointed Dr Claudio Ferrari, a Liverpool-based barrister who had once played for the Italian suitors, to represent them in negotiations with Everton. The proposed deal appeared to suit all three parties. Everton would bank a hefty £15,000 fee and offload an unhappy player without strengthening any English rivals. Roma would gain a classy, play-making centre-half who was well suited to the continental game. For T.G., the move promised international stardom, financial security and glorious Mediterranean sunshine. On offer were wages of £25 per week (more than tripling his Everton pay), luxury accommodation outside the city, a Lancia sports car, free flights to visit home and the promise of a coaching role after he retired from playing.

Confidence from all parties that the transfer would go through subsided in the weeks which followed, and the deal foundered. A 1962 Western Mail article intimated that T.G.'s financial demands were too great for Roma. However, the more widely accepted explanation is that red tape scuppered the deal. Only three years after the end of the Second World War, there was reluctance on the part of the British government and Everton to conduct business in Italian lire. Tommy recalled to Paul Joyce: 'Just before my wife and I were due to go, the [British] government stepped in and stopped the deal because they said the Italian lira was worthless.' At the end of August, Everton's board minutes noted that Roma could not source sufficient sterling to conclude the deal. Everton were willing to listen to offers from other interested clubs – Chelsea and Notts County were mentioned in the board minutes – but only if they matched the £15,000 agreed with Roma. None were willing to do so. So, instead of flying to a new life in the Italian capital, T.G. found himself on £8 per week, lining up at Goodison against Newcastle, when the 1948/49 season got under way.

The campaign started off in dire fashion; eighteen goals were conceded in a winless five-match streak. With the team in the relegation zone in October, the board finally elected to appoint a manager in the modern sense of the word rather than an administrator-cum-manager as Theo Kelly had been. Kelly resumed a purely secretarial role and former player Cliff Britton returned to the club as manager. Since retiring from playing at the end of the war, Britton had forged an impressive reputation in his first managerial post at Burnley – gaining promotion to the First Division and leading the team to an FA Cup Final. Negotiating with Everton's board from a position of strength, he insisted that he would have sole control of first-team affairs – an arrangement that had previously been anathema to the conservative directors. Near the top of Britton's in-tray was the T.G. Jones situation. Britton, after reviewing the squad, told the board that only T.G. was of the required quality for the top flight, so he was clearly keen to retain the centre-half's services. When they met, T.G. intimated that he would be prepared to come off the transfer list – tacitly confirming that the Italian dream had died.

Fifty years on, T.G. remained bitter about the collapse of the Roma deal – holding Everton at least partly responsible in spite of most evidence pointing to the club being happy to see him leave for Italy. When Torino moved to sign Dave Hickson from Everton in 1953, the bid was rejected without the 'Cannonball Kid' even being informed. T.G. could only look on enviously nine years after his collapsed transfer later when his countryman, John Charles, moved to Juventus and enjoyed fame and acclaim as Il Gigante Buono ('The Gentle Giant').

Putting the frustrations of the collapsed Roma transfer aside, T.G. rolled back the years to produce vintage form in the 1948/49 season – only the 1938/39 championship campaign saw him make more appearances. His resurgence could not have come at a better time as the club found itself fighting relegation for much of the season. With goals scored in short supply, T.G.'s coolness and organisational skills at the back became of paramount importance. Ever-present in the side from 30 November, he helped to steer the club to finish three places above the drop zone.

One young supporter attending Goodison Park and being star-struck by watching T.G. play in this era was Harold Matthews: 'There was no television in those days. We had the radio, football annuals, Sunday papers and cigarette cards. We knew every player in every team and the international players were like gods. I travelled to the ground with my mate via bus, ferryboat and tram and we were always amongst the first in. A small bottle of pop and jam butties in our pockets. Sometimes pop and a small malt loaf. The funny thing was, we weren't too bothered about the result. We went to see the stars, but our two main stars, Mercer and Lawton, had moved away. Our favourite Everton players were Ted Sagar, Nobby Fielding and T.G. Jones.

'From our front row spot we looked straight down the pitch and T.G. always seemed to be in the middle. We were only little kids and all I can remember is a guy who looked as big as Marouane Fellaini. He wasn't, of course, but that's how I remember him. A giant, elegant Robert Taylor lookalike with his dark wavy hair. T.G. displayed amazing balance as he moved effortlessly left and right, winning the ball with ease and having it under full control. Like Pirlo in a number five shirt, he was spraying passes with both feet all over the place. Unbeatable in the air, I wish we had him today.'

In the 1940s the centre-half considered to mirror T.G.'s playing style closest was Neil Franklin. Four years T.G.'s junior, and several inches shorter, Franklin eschewed an overtly physical approach to nullifying the threat from opposition forwards. Instead, he relied on his timing and football intelligence when playing for Stoke City and England. Evertonian Ray Terry was fortunate to see both play and makes this comparison: 'I saw Neil Franklin on several occasions. He became the regular centre-half in the England team after a number of other players had been tried following the retirement of Stan Cullis. As a player, he was a reasonably cultured type. He read the game well, was a good header of the ball and was sound and reliable defensively. Of recent players, he probably resembled Rio Ferdinand's style of play. I don't think he was as good an all-round player as T.G. and certainly didn't have the same power of shot.'

This period saw record attendances at grounds throughout the UK. Goodison Park's highest ever gate was recorded in September 1948 when Liverpool were the visitors. T.G. fondly recalled the Merseyside derby crowds: 'There were nearly eighty thousand people on the ground and not a fight anywhere. They were all standing up shoulder to shoulder… taking the mickey out of each other and enjoying every minute of it. I think this is how Liverpool developed its sense of humour. '(RT)

He got on well with one of his regular derby opponents, centre-forward Albert Stubbins: 'He was a great fellow. I used to like Albert very much, and he was a good player. Towards the end of one game somebody slotted this ball down the middle, and Albert turned, and do you know what? He'd covered six paces before I'd turned round. I couldn't catch him – no chance. God, he was like a racehorse.'(RT)

T.G. enjoyed the unique atmosphere of Merseyside derbies and the humorous exchanges with Reds: 'I can remember playing in a local derby at Liverpool. Most players in those days had their hair short-cropped but mine was always long. I remember being by the Kop and Liverpool had a corner. As I went to pick the ball up to kick it out to the corner, somebody threw a shilling, shouting, "Get your bloody hair cut!" [and] so I picked it up and put it in my pocket. I said, "Thank you very much," and do you know, it made me very popular with them, actually. In those days, I won't say Liverpool were a kick-and-a-rush side, but they played the long ball more than they played the short one. They were burly, hard players, whereas apart from Tommy Lawton and myself, we were only little chaps at Everton really, but they could move that ball about. There was no physical game at Everton, but Anfield, very definitely, yes.'(RT)

He would recount just how physical the game could be: 'The game was very, very hard – much harder and dirtier than it is now. There were a lot of dirty tricks practised. Going over the top was the worst thing – you had to be very skilled, very well practised, to really be effective at this, and ankle-tapping. And going in to head a ball where you'd miss it deliberately and get a fellow in the face – look at that nose of mine!'(RT) (T.G. bore the scar of a badly broken nose from a 1942 wartime fixture against Wolverhampton Wanderers.)

The season was rounded off in May 1949 with the first Welsh national team tour in foreign climes. Team manager Charlie Leyfield selected his erstwhile Everton teammate, T.G., to captain the side in defeats to Portugal, Belgium and Switzerland. T.G. was particularly impressed by the Portuguese coast. He sent a postcard from the resort of Estoril back to Joyce, who was staying in Hoylake with the Mercers. It read, 'You can see by the photo overleaf what sort of place this is, need I say more? The weather is perfect, only too hot to sunbathe. Have been to Lisbon today, everything is so expensive. You should see the fashions!'

T.G.'s pivotal contribution to maintaining Everton's top-flight status in the 1948/49 season was recognised with the long-overdue award of club captaincy at the expense of Peter Farrell. To the outside observer it appeared that peace had been restored between T.G. and the club after the publicly aired bickering of the previous three years. However, this positive development masked a deteriorating relationship between manager and player. On returning to the club, Cliff Britton had insisted that his former playing colleagues, such as T.G. and Norman Greenhalgh, address him as 'Mr Britton' rather than 'Cliff'. This was Britton's way of distancing himself from his former peers – an understandable desire but also a source of irritation to those he had previously been on first-name terms with. With the club's spending budget diminished, Britton and the directors were also committed to bringing local talent through the ranks, rather than acquiring established stars to fill the gap left by the departures of Tommy Lawton, Joe Mercer, Torry Gillick and others.

With confidence and ego emboldened by hero-worship from the terraces, T.G. was disinclined to pay heed to the higher echelons of the club. The newly created position of team manager was an alien concept to long-serving players, who were accustomed to devising their own tactics and imparting guidance to their younger teammates. Trainers focused on fitness regimes, as T.G. explained: 'Our trainer was an old man, Harry Cooke – a great fellow. He was better at doing the boots and things like that – keeping peace in the camp. He was more like a supervisor than a trainer. We had Theo Kelly as secretary-manager; Theo had never played football. The players taught the players. In the dressing room they said, "Don't you do that again." For instance, if I gave a pass and it went to the opposition, they were on me like a ton of bricks, and if I did it twice, I wasn't in the team the next week. It was that important to keep the ball in your own possession. You saw what they did and you automatically did the same thing. You discarded the poor things and encouraged the good things. It's coaching, in my mind, of the very best kind. The professionals did it all, they talked to each other and they understood each other, and I think this is the most important aspect of the game.'[RT]

Having a new figure calling the shots – especially one who had once been a teammate – grated with T.G. He reminisced: 'They appointed Cliff Britton as manager… that was the first time that tactics and a new system were devised and discussed at Everton. Cliff used to get them together [and say], "This is how we're going to play."'[RT] T.G., supremely confident in his own abilities – to the point of arrogance – was increasingly reticent to be told what to do or how to play. He would reflect on his unshakeable belief in his cultured, unflappable, playing style to journalist George Harrison in 1974: 'I was never one for clearing the lines by booting [the ball] anywhere. I preferred to get the ball, hold it, then start our forwards moving, even if it happened in our own box. It might have given folks in the stands near heart-failure at times, but I very rarely lost the ball under pressure.'[DP]

The 1949/50 season started promisingly with two consecutive wins. Stork's report of the first game, a 1–0 victory over Middlesbrough, showed that the captaincy had not tempered T.G.'s showmanship: 'There was a tense moment in front of the Everton goal when Jones tried to work the "dummy" on Corr. The move failed to come off, and it left the Everton goal in rather a perilous position.'[FE] In spite of Everton being brought back down to earth with a heavy defeat at Newcastle, the Daily Post was full of praise for the captain: 'Tommy Jones was the best man on the field. He held Milburn effectively and got his backs and goalkeeper out of many difficult situations. Even from the press box one could hear him trying to rally his men in the second half.'

Things quickly turned sour. A 0–7 collapse to Portsmouth at Fratton Park was described by observers as one of the worst team performances in living memory. Following this defeat, Britton opted for a pragmatic, risk-averse style of play. He called T.G. into his office to advise him of this – it was not well received by a player unwilling to compromise his expansive method of play. T.G. recalled Britton's words at the meeting: 'He said, "Look, I want this dribbling in the penalty box cut out. Some of the directors are getting heart failure." This was Cliff Britton, the man whose ball control was renowned in his day, and he told me this. I said, "I can't play any other way, Cliff." And then he said, "You've got to; I want this ball booted out of the penalty box." So in the next match I went on and I kicked the ball all over the park, and the press came out with: "What happened, what was this?" It was so foreign. The Evertonians came to see people like me playing football, that's what they wanted. When I started to play like a third-rater,

Cliff Britton was on me like a ton of bricks, saying: "You've made me look a fool." [So] I said, "But that's what you wanted. You told me to."[RT]

T.G.'s nephew, Chris Kozlowski, remembers T.G. recounting an exchange with Britton: 'I remember once talking to T.G. He said he used to defend by taking the ball across his own goal and was told off by the manager even though they had won: "You almost got us into trouble there, Tom," to which he replied, "Let me know when I do."'

In mid-October, T.G. was selected to represent Wales against England at Ninian Park. In his absence, Jack Humphreys was restored to the Everton first team. After playing in the 4–1 defeat to England, T.G. returned to Everton and was selected to captain the side facing Southport in a midweek Liverpool Senior Cup tie. This competition only enjoyed a modest status, but nonetheless the 1–3 home defeat was embarrassing, with T.G. at fault for at least one of the goals. Pilot noted: 'Tommy Jones seemed quite at a loss against the fast-moving forwards.'[EE] In spite of this aberration, T.G. travelled down to St Andrews on the following Saturday with every expectation that he would line up against Birmingham City in the league fixture. It proved to be a fateful afternoon: 'I was captain of the team and used to take talks and things like that, which was my job. We were in the hotel before the match in Birmingham, and we were having our talk. Cliff Britton always insisted on us having our talks, and, as usual, I took control of the players. After this was finished he called me over. "Listen," he said, "you've embarrassed me." I said, "Why? What have I done now?" He said, "I wasn't going to play you this afternoon… [Humphreys] played well, so I was going to leave you out and play him."

'Well, I felt dreadfully hurt, because I'd considered that Ted Sagar and I were the two chaps in the side who were holding them together at this time. We had a very, very poor side. They'd brought all these players in who I considered, quite honestly, to be third-raters who were not good enough for a club like Everton. Anyway, I was so angry, I caught the next train home – I didn't even see the match. And that was the beginning of the end for me at Everton.'[RT]

T.G.'s deselection made headlines in the Merseyside sports press. Leslie Edwards reported a slightly different timetable of events:

Thirty minutes before the match Humphreys was told to

strip and Jones was told he would not be required. So Jones'
experience in a short eight days took in an international ap-
pearance at Cardiff, a semi-reserve team appearance against
Southport in midweek and a place in the stand at St Andrews
– a shattering experience. The Everton view, I believe, is that
Humphreys played well enough against Bolton to justify his
further inclusion. Whether Jones will be content to play Cen-
tral League football with Everton is something which can be
answered only by the player. (DP)

Britton was a football purist as a player but, in the trying circumstances Everton found themselves in, he believed that Humphreys' traditional centre-half approach was preferable to that of the more aesthetically pleasing T.G. A personality
clash may also have been at the root of the schism. The two had never been close
as teammates and it appears that Britton felt that T.G., through over-elaboration
on the field, was playing for himself rather than the relegation-threatened team.
In unpublished memoirs, written in the early 1970s, Britton alluded to his former
teammate:

Not every star player is prepared to conduct himself in a man-
ner which is in the best interests of the team. This can lead to
a test of strength between the player and the manager, with
the rest of the team as onlookers. It is an unenviable position
for any manager to be in but, to retain the respect of his play-
ers, it is a battle he dare not lose.

Rather than be faced with such a confrontation some manag-
ers prefer players of lesser ability with more stable characters
on which to build his team. Players who lack a sense of re-
sponsibility to themselves are not thought, by some managers,
to be the best ones in whose hands to place their livelihood.

Henceforth, T.G. found himself frozen out of the first team, his pride badly
hurt. He told Paul Joyce in 1997: 'From being captain of Everton and Wales I
went to nothing. They wouldn't even play me in the reserves.' (LE) He elaborated
on the situation he found himself in during the autumn of 1949 when interviewed by Rogan Taylor: 'Cliff Britton wouldn't play me in the first team and he

wouldn't play me in the reserves. You see, I was tremendously popular at Everton then, and if they [the supporters] had seen me playing in the reserves, they would have known I wasn't injured. But by not being played at all, there was an excuse to put somebody else in, and say that I was injured.'[RT]

Denied his football fix at Goodison, T.G. sought it in the most unlikely of surroundings. Decades later, he would chuckle when recalling how he moonlighted under the nose of Everton: 'I'm going to tell you something now that you really will hardly believe. All the players should have turned up at Everton for home matches, including those who weren't playing. I used to play on Saturdays for Hawarden Grammar School Old Boys, and I was captain of Wales and captain of Everton! I actually played my last game for Wales, against Belgium at Cardiff, which we won, on a Wednesday. I actually played at Bangor for Hawarden Grammar School Old Boys against Bangor University on the Saturday before.'[RT]

Through a friendship with the Old Boys' fixture secretary, Nigel Wright, T.G. had previously turned out for the team in a pre-season friendly match against Connah's Quay Juniors. With Everton playing at Chelsea on 19 November, T.G. appeared at left-half for the Old Boys in a fixture against Bangor University. Obligingly, the Leader and Chester Chronicle match reports listed the ringer in the ranks as 'A. Williams'. 'Williams' was reported to have been 'outstanding' in defence during the 3–1 victory.

T.G. would later joke about his impact on the attendances at Hawarden's games: 'They had pretty good gates when the word got around!' With Humphreys injured, T.G. was recalled to Everton's first team as the 1949 festive season approached.

Recalled for the Christmas Eve derby at Anfield, T.G. retained his place for the Boxing Day home fixture against Fulham. The match ended in a 1–1 draw. In what would be his final first-team appearance for Everton T.G. conceded a penalty for an 'inexplicable' handball. Just four days later, Everton's board agreed with Cliff Britton that T.G. should be made available for transfer, but only at an acceptable price.

Word of the impasse between club and player reached the Llyn Peninsula in northwest Wales. A new chapter in T.G.'s life, away from Goodison Park, was about to begin.

7

PRINCE OF PWLLHELI

IN THE SUMMER OF 1949, T.G. HAD HOLIDAYED WITH JOYCE
on the Llyn Peninsula. In this rural, predominantly Welsh-speaking region, the
presence of the captain of the national football team must have turned heads.
The press coverage of T.G.'s seemingly never-ending quest to escape from
Goodison planted the germ of an idea in the minds of prominent people in the
coastal town of Pwllheli.

Chief among them was Thomas Morris 'T.M.' Jones, a businessman with
interests in hotels, farming and road haulage. He had become acquainted with
Merseyside during the Second World War when his lorries transported rabbits
and other produce from the Llyn Peninsula to help feed people in Liverpool and
its hinterland. A keen sports follower and Evertonian, T.M. held a season ticket at
Goodison Park and would have been acutely aware of the clouds gathering over
T.G.'s footballing future. With his close friend and GP, Dr Idris Jones (known as
'Doc'), T.M. Jones devised an audacious plan to offer T.G. a lucrative escape route
from Everton and English football. In early February 1950, a two-car delegation

T.G., wearing a cap, pictured with his younger siblings in approximately 1926. Courtesy of Ceris Jones.

T.G. wearing a Welsh schoolboy international cap, awarded in 1932. Courtesy of Jane Jones.

T.G. photographed around the time of his transfer from Wrexham to Everton in 1936. Courtesy of Ceris Jones.

T.G.'s first appearance in an Everton squad photo (back row, third from right) – prior to the start of the 1936-37 season. Next to him is Ted Sagar. Courtesy of John Rowlands.

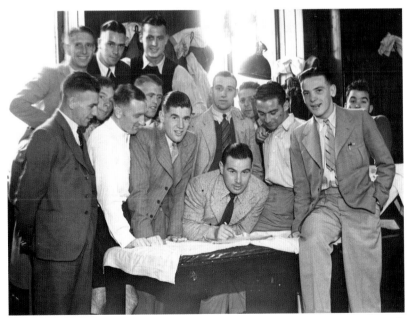

Everton's players are all smiles as they clock-in at the start of pre-season training in 1937. T.G. is on Billy Cook's shoulder as he signs the registration book. Partly obscured, "Dixie" Dean, entering his final season at the club, looks on from the rear. Courtesy of John Rowlands.

United nations of Everton. Billy Cook (Ireland), Albert Geldard (England), Jock Thomson (Scotland) and T.G. Jones (Wales) are photographed training for the Empire Exhibition Tournament at Hampden Park in the spring of 1938. Geldard would leave Everton for Bolton Wanderers shortly afterwards. Courtesy of John Rowlands.

Everton's players having fun on a summer European tour in the late 1930s (T.G. is second from left). Courtesy of Jane Jones.

The Everton squad, photographed shortly after winning the league title in 1939. Standing (L-R): Harry Cooke (trainer), Jock Thomson (captain), Gordon Watson, Billy Cook (vice-captain), Ted Sagar, Joe Mercer, Norman Greenhalgh, T.G. Jones. Seated (L-R): Torry Gillick, Stan Bentham, Tommy Lawton, Alex Stevenson, Wally Boyes, Jimmy Caskie. Courtesy of Jane Jones.

T.G., by now an established first-teamer at Everton, poses for a Topical Times portrait in the summer of 1938.

Joe Mercer, Tommy Lawton, Jimmy Caskie, Gordon Watson and T.G. at Goodison Park, contemplating what the future holds after war is declared in September 1939. Courtesy of the Watson family.

Like most of his teammates, T.G. served as a wartime physical training instructor in the forces. He is pictured here with colleagues in the RAF. Courtesy of Jane Jones.

T.G. proudly leads out the Welsh football team prior to a match with England at Wembley on 25 September 1943. England ran out comfortable winners, 8-3.

Before a Merseyside derby on 10 April 1944, Everton's pre-war squad were reunited as chairman W.C. Gibbins presented long-service 'benefit' payments. T.G. looks on as Wally Boyes receives his cheque. Courtesy of David Wright.

T.G. and Joyce on their Isle of Man honeymoon in 1945. Courtesy of Jane Jones.

T.G. and Joyce photographed around the time of their marriage. Courtesy of Jane Jones.

Everton's squad which sought to defend the league title won in 1939. Tommy Lawton had departed in 1945 and Joe Mercer (second from left, back row) would depart for Arsenal during the course of the season. Courtesy of Jane Jones.

T.G. and Gordon Watson (6) challenge an opposition forward in a post-war match staged at Goodison Park. Courtesy of Brendan Connolly.

Easter Monday 1948. T.G. outleaps the goalkeeper and heads for the Grimsby Town goal at the Gwladys Street End. Jackie Grant (7) and Jock Dodds (9) look on. T.G. rated Dodds as one of the hardest forwards to play against in wartime football. Courtesy of Jane Jones.

T.G. giving a football lecture at a TJ Hughes store in Liverpool in June 1948. He enjoyed imparting his sporting wisdom and coached teenagers on behalf of the Liverpool County F.A. Courtesy of Mark Thomas.

Connah's Quay Juniors' committee for the 1947-48 season included, in its ranks, T.G. (back row far right) and fellow former Welsh international Billy Hughes (back row third from left). Source: Juniors to Nomads.

T.G. captained his national team on its first European tour. He is pictured here at the pre-match handshake with the Portugese captain in Lisbon. Courtesy of Wrexham County Borough Museum and Archive.

CONNAH'S QUAY JUNIORS F.C.

ATTRACTIVE FOOTBALL MATCH

on the

HALF WAY
GROUND

on

MONDAY, AUGUST 29th

T. G. JONES'
SELECTED XI

v.

EVERTON A

who will include several prominent players

Kick-off 7 p.m.   Admission 1/-   Ladies 6d   Children 3d

All to pay

W. Fewster & Sons, Ltd., Printers, Connah's Quay

*T.G. helped stage a number of friendly matches at Connah's Quay Juniors' Half Way Ground. On this occasion in 1949 he used his influence to get Everton's third team to visit his hometown.
Courtesy of Jimmy Harris.*

Tommy Lawton came to stay at T.G.'s Tower Hotel in Pwllheli. He spent much of his holiday trying, without success, to persuade T.G. to join him at Notts County. Courtesy of Jane Jones.

Elizabeth Jones helps out at the bar in the Tower Hotel, supervised by her proud father, looking immaculate, as usual. Courtesy of Jane Jones.

Joe Mercer, accompanied by his son, David, receives congratulations from his friend, T.G. The occasion may have been Mercer winning the FA Cup with Arsenal in 1950. Courtesy of Jane Jones.

The Jones and Mercer families would holiday together. T.G. indulges in sunbathing, seemingly oblivious to the camera whilst the others look on. Courtesy of Jane Jones.

T.G. spent seven seasons with Pwllheli and District FC, leading them to unheralded success. Courtesy of Bernie Smith.

T.G. watches on as his goalkeeper clear the ball under pressure from opposition forwards at the Recreation Ground. Courtesy of Bernie Smith.

T.G.'s status and the Pwllheli team's success brought the crowds flooding to the Recreation Ground, as evidenced by this photo taken in 1952. Courtesy of Bernie Smith.

Supporters surround T.G. as he holds the 1951/52 league champions' trophy aloft at Pwll-heli's Recreation Ground. Courtesy of Bernie Smith.

T.G. clasps the league champion-ship trophy having secured the 1951/52 Welsh League North title in an away fixture at Porthmadog. Courtesy of Jane Jones.

T.G. in an aerial duel from a corner at Rhyl during a Welsh Cup tie. Courtesy of Bernie Smith.

A caricature by Ralph in The Herald of Wales, depicting T.G. as Pwllheli's puppet master on the pitch.

The manager, photographed in the 1950s. Courtesy of Jane Jones.

TG and Bangor City goalkeeper
Ifor Roberts 'have words' during
a match at Farrar Road against
Port Vale.
Courtesy of Ifor Roberts.

T.G. delivers a team talk to his
Bangor City players in 1962.
Standing (L-R): T.G., Emyr
Ab Iorwerth, Barry Wilkinson,
Ken Birch, Brian Ellis, Eddy
Murphy. Seated (L-R): Len
Davies and Bill Souter.
Courtesy of Dafydd ab Iorwerth.

Bangor City players celebrate
in the bath having beaten
Wrexham in the 1962 Welsh
Cup final.
Courtesy of the Birch family.

The Hornet comic commemorates Bangor City's cup feats in 1962. Courtesy of the Birch family.

T.G. with daughter Elizabeth at her wedding in 1974. Courtesy of Jane Jones.

Young Everton supporters call in at T.G's shop near Bangor Pier in the summer of 1995. Courtesy of Phil Parker.

A sad day for T.G. The newspaper shop closes after 30 years in the Jones family's ownership. Well-wishers' cards and flowers decorate the front window. Courtesy of Jane Jones.

In April 2017 T.G.'s relatives join gap Connah's Quay Nomads' Director of Football, Jay Catton, as T.G. becomes an inaugural inductee into the club's Hall of Fame. Courtesy of Nik Mesney.

T.G.'s induction into the Hall of Fame is commemorated on gap Connah's Quay Nomads' clubhouse wall. Courtesy of Nik Mesney.

left Pwllheli and headed east for Connah's Quay. T.M. Jones was accompanied in his Standard Vanguard by Dafydd Morris Jones (his son) and Dr Idris Jones. In the second car were Lyn Hughes (a coalman) and Robert Dafydd Griffith (a plumber).

Arriving at T.G.'s home, the offer was laid on the table. The Pwllheli Tower Hotel had been purchased for £12,000 from Lord Newborough by T.M. Jones, Dr Jones and a local farmer, Mervyn Jones, with the intention of persuading T.G. to become its proprietor. The hotel dated back to the seventeenth century and, with an imposing position on Pwllheli's high street, was the top establishment in the town. It was popular with businessmen and holidaymakers, and used for black-tie functions. Although not central to the proposal, T.G. was also given the option of earning additional income by playing for Pwllheli and District Football Club, of which T.M. Jones and Dr Jones were directors.

In 2004, Dafydd Morris Jones told journalist Ioan Jones about that meeting with T.G. 'We had a great welcome from Tommy – he took us to Everton to see Goodison Park. They told him about the offer and left him to think about it.'

In light of the irrevocable breakdown in his relationship with Cliff Britton and the Everton board, the proposal was deemed worthy of T.G.'s consideration. Even an injury to Jack Humphreys did not open a way back into the first team. Ted Falder – ironically a former RAF colleague for whom T.G. had arranged an Everton trial – wore the number 5 shirt for the remainder of the season. T.G. believed that the Everton board's intransigence over the transfer fee would deter other top-flight teams from signing him – a release on a free transfer was not being countenanced. However, the thought of walking away from top-level football must have been unappetising when there was every likelihood that he could continue playing at a high level of the game for several more years. He recalled: 'I could have gone on playing for Everton till I was 35 or 36 or more, because I used to play the game without any great effort. I used to read the game... But you see, my days at Everton were numbered.'[RT]

News of the Pwllheli proposal broke in the Merseyside press on 14 February. When asked for comment, the Everton chairman, Cecil Baxter, responded: 'Jones has said nothing to us about the possibility of going out of league football. The position is that he is still on the transfer list at his own request. Up to date, there have been no offers for him. Whether the deadline date of signings, March 6, will bring anything further, I do not know.'

A week later, T.G. notified the club that he was accepting the proposal to become a hotelier. Reluctant, however, to turn away from league football completely, he tabled a compromise proposal whereby he would make himself available to Everton solely on weekends during the following 1950/51 season. The offer received short shrift from Cliff Britton, thus sealing T.G.'s Everton exit after a fourteen-year stay. T.G. and Joyce officially took tenancy of the Tower Hotel on 20 March 1950. Thus was born one of his Welsh nicknames: Twm Tŵr – 'Tom of the Tower'. His friend, Nigel Wright, would send him the Chester and Deeside newspapers each week so that he could keep abreast of news from his hometown. T.G. made himself available to return to Merseyside at weekends for the remainder of the football season but he was never called upon to play for the first team. The Caernarvon and Denbigh Herald reported: 'Whilst regretting the end of his senior football career the offer of the business was so attractive – securing his future – that it was impossible to turn down. Mr Jones, in an interview, said: "The business transaction has, in no way, any connection with football."'

The move caused a sensation in North Wales. Strained relations with Everton proved no barrier to T.G. arranging a friendly match at Pwllheli's Recreation Ground (known locally as 'The Rec') on 19 April. The Everton XI was essentially a youth team containing future first-teamers Albert Dunlop, Dan Donovan and Tony McNamara. The right-back that day, Thomas Edwin 'T.E.' Jones, would succeed T.G. as Everton's centre-half the following season. Although no match for T.G. in terms of ability, T.E. would prove to be a fine servant to the club – captaining the first team for much of the late 1950s. Looking back, he reflected on the difficulties of following in the footsteps of a club legend:

> *Because of my name and the position I was playing in, I had difficulty when I broke through to the side. People kept comparing me with T.G. Jones. The truth is that I couldn't compare with T.G., he was a brilliant player. I first played with him when I was in the reserves at sixteen. I was a right full-back and he was a centre-half. He played the ball to me and I hit, what I thought was, a good pass down the line to our outside-right. T.G. wasn't too impressed. He gave me a*

right rollicking because he had wanted me to play the ball
back to him, even though he was on the edge of our penalty
area. He was a great player with fantastic ability. You couldn't
emulate anybody like T.G. He had such confidence in his
ability that there was no situation that was too tight for him,
and he was always so cool. I could never copy his style, it was
unique. I just played the game as I thought I could play it. [EP]

'Offside', of the Caernarvon and Denbigh Herald, reported on the 3–2 victory for the visitors, a match which would be T.G.'s farewell Everton appearance:

For the first twenty minutes the speed of the Evertonians
baffled the homesters. T.G. Jones was the master tactician
and he kept his forwards well-fed with accurate passes. Ever-
ton played very open football, switching the ball from wing to
wing and delighting the crowd with very neat inter-passing
movements. Pwllheli were very good individually but lacked
cohesion.

The after-match reception was held, unsurprisingly, at the Tower Hotel. Toasts and speeches were exchanged between the clubs, with T.G. responding on behalf of the Everton players. The imposing hotel would play host to several of T.G.'s football friends over his seven years as proprietor. Joe Mercer, Tommy Lawton and Ron Burgess would all be photographed visiting the establishment. Lawton spent a fortnight at the Tower Hotel trying to convince T.G. to return to professional football by joining him at Brentford, where the striker had become player-manager. T.G.'s nephew, Chris Kozlowski, remembers his childhood impressions of the hotel: 'It seemed to us kids to be huge, with three or four floors. It had a rear courtyard and old stables. There was a large spiral staircase with a thick wood banister which we were tempted to slide down but were forbidden to, except for the last six feet.'

Over on Merseyside, Everton limped to an eighteenth-place finish – three places above the relegation zone. T.G.'s final appearance at Goodison Park was in a reserve fixture against Sheffield United on 18 March 1950, but his shadow rested on the shoulders of Everton centre-halves for decades to come.

On 6 May 1950, Everton's season ended at home to already-relegated Manchester City. It was billed as a celebration of Ted Sagar's service to the club as he was recalled to make his 430th appearance. In his match preview, the Liverpool Echo's Ranger bemoaned the absence of another Goodison great:

> *The inclusion of Sagar is Everton's only change. One other alteration that many staunch Evertonians would like to have seen would have been the inclusion of Tommy Jones, so that the Welsh international could have been given a fitting farewell by his many admirers. Jones' service may not have been as long as Sagar's but he, too, has been a wonderful ornament to the game, and still remains implanted in my mind as the finest centre-half I have ever seen. It would have been nice to see him in action for the last time in Everton's colours.*

As Everton kicked off the match at Goodison Park, eighty miles away T.G. was donning the white of Pwllheli for the first time, in a friendly match. Fittingly, it was against his first club, Wrexham. Gate receipts totalled £156 at the Rec as a large crowd witnessed a 1-0 victory for the home team.

> *T.G. Jones was cool and broke up many movements which looked dangerous. The second half was not ten minutes old when Pwllheli were awarded a free-kick. T.G. Jones took the kick and scored with a terrific drive. This goal delighted the crowd... In this half we saw T.G. Jones the tactician – what a difference T.G. made to the team. He was brilliant, cool and managed to inspire the whole team.*[CDH]

At the 1950 Pwllheli and District FC AGM, held on 2 June, it was confirmed that T.G. would play for the team, but he sought to downplay reports that he would captain and coach the side: 'I am simply going to play for the team.' The North Wales Chronicle reported that T.G. had turned down a long-term contract to coach the side, with Les Boulter, the former Charlton Athletic and Wales player, agreeing to assist as required. Boulter had previously combined the role of Pwllheli's player-manager with running a local sweetshop. As things transpired, T.G. did become the kingpin of the club, captaining and coaching the team throughout his tenure. Wage slips reveal that T.G. was receiving £10 per week to play for Pwllheli, nearly double that awarded to his highest-paid teammates and more than he earned as an Everton player.

Everton retained T.G.'s playing registration in the hope that a fee might be recouped should he eventually be lured to a Football League club. In late July, Third Division Notts County approached T.G. in the hope of tempting him back to English football by reuniting him with Tommy Lawton. A £5,000 transfer fee was mooted but T.G. notified Everton, by phone, that he was electing to focus on his hotel business. Shorn of T.G.'s services, Everton continued on a downward trajectory the following season – enduring the ignominy of relegation for only the second time in the club's history in May 1951. He recalled: 'Fifteen years later, I rang Everton and I said, "Am I still on the transfer list?" They said, "Yes"!'[RT]

Looking back more than forty years after his exit from Goodison Park, T.G.'s rancour had not subsided. He told Andy Morris: 'In those days, contracts were weighed against a player, and when I left Everton I couldn't play for another [Football] League team. It ruined my career and I'll never forgive the club.'[DP]

It seems appropriate that T.G.'s departure from English football coincided with that of Neil Franklin, another great centre-half. However, the Stoke pivot was bound for far more exotic climes. Having turned down the latest terms offered by Stoke, he made a flit to sign for Santa Fe of Bogota, in a league not recognised by FIFA. Several others crossed the Atlantic to enjoy the riches on offer, notably Manchester United's Charlie Mitten. Whereas T.G. resisted overtures to return to the Football League, homesickness brought Franklin home within weeks of embarking on his Colombian adventure. On his return, he found himself ostracised by the football establishment. Top-flight clubs showed no interest in signing him, so he resumed his career with Second Division Hull City. He was never selected to represent his country again – Wolves' Billy Wright being the long-term beneficiary.

Pwllheli and District FC competed in the Welsh League North, Division One, against the likes of Porthmadog, Colwyn Bay and Holyhead Town. North Wales' larger clubs, such as Wrexham, Bangor City and Rhyl, competed in the English league structure, but fielded reserve teams in the Welsh League. Although the presence of former Football League players on generous salaries would become a feature of the North Wales football scene – leading to it being humorously referred to as the Gold Coast – the arrival of the former Everton and Wales captain was the most significant and astonishing of all. T.G. inherited a strong squad containing semi-pro players and several amateurs who would be stalwarts in his time at the club. Among them were Matt Matthews, Gordon Gerrard, free-scoring centre-forward Aaron 'Mac' Enyon, and flying left-winger George Makin – who had, in fact, been a wartime Everton clubmate of T.G. He set about blending them with key signings like Vince Pritchard to create a formidable unit capable of delivering the club's first league title.

The local council, who owned the Rec, offered the club a long-term lease of the ground and provided a 250-seat stand to complement a 500-capacity covered standing area provided by the supporters' club. All other spectators stood around the pitch behind ropes. T.G.'s league debut, against Flint Town United, saw Pwllheli get the 1950/51 season off to a winning start. The season reached its crescendo on the final day, 10 May 1951, when 4,200 spectators crowded into the Rec. Victory over Holyhead Town would be enough to secure the league title on goal average from Conwy. With thirteen minutes left, the match was goalless, but a rapid burst of two goals from Pwllheli – the latter a solo effort from Vince Pritchard – seemed to have seen the home side to safety. After a late Holyhead penalty, though, the home team had to cling on until the final whistle, whereupon the fans invaded pitch and chaired the players off.

The 1951/52 season was triumphant as T.G.'s team swept aside opponents, averaging four goals scored per match. As the season neared its conclusion the team was bolstered by the temporary enlistment of Ken Hodgkisson and Gordon Nutt of West Bromwich Albion and Coventry City, respectively. The pair were posted on their national service to the Tonfanau military camp when recruited by T.G. Their talent and fresh legs proved invaluable during a late-season flurry of fixtures caused by the often unplayable state of pitches during the winter months. Unbeaten Pwllheli had already secured the title by fifteen points when T.G. was obliged to field a weakened team, largely consisting of schoolboys, in the final match of the league season. The dead rubber, a 9–0 loss to Blaenau Ffestiniog, did not prevent the 'Invincibles' moniker being given to the team – a wry nod to the undefeated Preston North End team of the 1888/89 season. In the league the team had won 27, drawn four and lost just one, with a positive goal difference of 82. The senior players returned to action the next day for the Alves Cup Final, played against Llandudno FC, at Bangor City's Farrar Road ground. The tie saw two former Everton and Wales centre-halves on the pitch. Lining up against T.G. in the Llandudno number 5 shirt was Jack Humphreys, who would tragically succumb to tuberculosis a little over two years later. In a connection to Everton's future, Llandudno's Morrey brothers – Billy and Bernie – were to become the grandfather and great-uncle, respectively, of Wayne Rooney.

With Pwllheli weakened by the barrage of fixtures in the preceding week, Llandudno offered a stern test. It was T.G. who, almost single-handedly, kept his team in the match: 'One man alone saved Pwllheli and that was former Everton star and Welsh international Tom Jones. He simply blocked the passage down the middle to the Pwllheli goal by his cool and methodical play. He was at the right place at the right moment every time.'[(CDH)]

T.G.'s defensive efforts could not prevent Pwllheli trailing 0–1 until he equalised from the penalty spot with five minutes of regular time remaining. Aaron Enyon then hit the winner in extra time to secure the treble (the Cookson Cup was also won, while Pwllheli fell at the final hurdle in the North Wales Coast Challenge Cup). T.G. nearly capped the victory over Llandudno with a sensational strike: 'Just on time, from fully twenty yards outside the penalty area, Jones sent in a powerful shot. The ball simply flew from his boot and with goalkeeper Henderson beaten it crashed against the bar and rebounded almost back to the centre of the field.'[(CDH)]

The unforgettable, unsurpassable, season was celebrated with a civic reception held at Pwllheli's Crown Hotel with the mayor of the town presiding.

Keeping goal in that golden season was John Cowell. He recalls what it was like playing under and alongside the former Everton star: 'T.G. signed me. I was at university in Bangor and, unbeknown to me, he must have been watching one or two of our Wednesday games. The next thing was I got the knock at the door and Tommy was there himself. It was a huge honour for me, I was the only amateur – the rest were part-time professionals. I used to get three pounds per match despite being an amateur. Had the Football Association of Wales found out, I could have been suspended for life. Some of the part-time pros were only on six pounds. T.G. always played centre-half. He dominated and dictated the box completely. One can use all sorts of superlatives. He was outstanding – a complete footballer – there's no doubt about that. He could dribble the ball out of the box and was a remarkable header of the ball – unbeatable in the air. Today we'd be talking about a twenty- to thirty-million-pound valuation for him.

'He had a tremendous personality – he was the sort of fellow that if he walked into a room everybody stopped to look at him. He could be very brutal in his remarks in the dressing room but that was Tommy.'

In the book, Coast of Soccer Memories, Cowell added further praise: 'The kingpin of the team was Tommy himself, who not only stamped his personality on all those around him but always led by example. He was graceful, stylish, superb in judgement and position, and had all the qualities of genius.'

Such praise for T.G. was commonplace. Ernest Williams, who played for Pwllheli towards the end of T.G.'s time there, can recall both his ability and vanity: 'T.G. looked the part. He was very fastidious about his on-field and off-field appearance. Even in the lowly North Wales League he believed (although I never heard him say this) that if he walked on to the field looking as if he had come out of a beauty parlour he would already have won the battle of who was the most important player on the pitch – the rest were extras in the cast.

'Whereas most players kick a dead ball or free kick from a slight angle, he had this uncanny knack of attacking the ball straight on with tremendous extension of his right leg. In an era when the first aim of a defender was to hoof the ball as far as possible, he said to me, "Always make sure you pass the ball from defence and so retain possession."

'If it was a very windy day the ball was often soaked in a bucket of water before kick-off and to head such a ball was very painful. He told me that the secret was to make sure your feet were off the ground as you made contact as this would lessen the shock – it still hurt though!'

The impact of having a national sporting hero turning out in the Welsh League should not be underestimated. Young spectator Emyr Evans recalls the indelible mark T.G. made on his childhood: 'One of our regular Saturday trips from Anglesey was to Uncle Dick and Auntie Nel's house at Porthmadog. On one particular Saturday, Uncle Dick orchestrated a visit to Pwllheli to see the local Welsh League derby between a high-flying Porthmadog team and a Pwllheli side led by someone called "Tommy Jones", who I hadn't heard of previously, but who obviously created quite some excitement. When we arrived at the match the crowd seemed to be at least ten deep to the line, and I remember being passed to the front so that I could see the game. Although I can't remember the score, I can still see that tall dark-haired figure commanding the centre of defence. He seemed to attract the ball to him and when he had it, made unerring short and long passes to his less-talented teammates. I couldn't take my eyes off him. The terrific sense of "presence" emanating from him stays with me to this day.'

Pwllheli would never again hit the heights of those first two seasons under T.G., but would remain competitive in the higher echelons of the Welsh League North. With other clubs eroding Pwllheli's financial advantage, and budgets tightening, T.G. scouted and signed more local players, such as teenage half-back Hubert Hughes and Jack Murray, and mixed amateurs with semi-professionals – often hailing from Merseyside. Two notable acquisitions in 1953 were pugnacious full-backs Orig Williams and Idris Evans. Evans, a Nefyn plasterer by trade, had an aggressive style of play which earned him the nickname Tarw Nefyn ('The Nefyn Bull'). The equally combative Orig Williams was a larger-than-life character who went on to become a professional wrestler, prominent Welsh nationalist, broadcaster and journalist. Having had short spells at Oldham Athletic and Shrewsbury Town, Williams, a window cleaner, was hospitalised with a suspected blood clot on the brain. The doctor's orders were clear: 'You must never play football again.' Having been sought by T.G., Williams was able to secure medical clearance to resume his playing career alongside a man he had grown up reading about in the sports columns of newspapers.

Fixing up employment and accommodation for prospective signings was used as a recruiting tactic by T.G. at Pwllheli, and in later years at Bangor City. Williams was set up with a maintenance position at Butlin's holiday resort, located close to the town. In his autobiography, El Bandito, Williams emphasised T.G.'s contempt for authority – a throwback to his battles with Everton officials:

> He was, as you'd expect, immensely knowledgeable about patterns of play and how to adjust to situations and opponents. He wouldn't entertain slouches and those who wouldn't listen. He had no respect for authority either, especially the Football Association of Wales (FAW)… I remember one FAW official entering the Pwllheli dressing room at half-time when Tommy was having a rant. The big-wig had barely opened

his mouth before Tommy told him to 'piss off'.

Williams and Idris Evans became a feared defensive pairing in support of T.G. They were his disciples, and Williams credited the manager with bringing more than just brawn to their game:

> *He taught us how to tackle, retain and distribute. The man knew his stuff and we were more than willing pupils. Tommy could read the game and we were his two bookends. He was not short of a sharp word either. 'Orig,' he once told me, 'if that winger walks off the field at the end of this game you are a bloody coward.'*

By the autumn of 1953, Ifor Roberts had succeeded John Cowell in goal. Roberts would get to know T.G. better than most other players as he was frequently given lifts to matches by the manager. He recalls what it was like meeting and playing alongside a boyhood hero: 'I was taken as a little kid to Goodison to see Everton. Being a goalkeeper, I was looking to see Ted Sagar, but the supporters' adulation was for T.G. Jones – you have never seen such adulation in your life. He became a hero for me. I saw this colossal man with such artistry – the crowd would urge him upfield for every corner. Some players would just go up there for the sake of it but he would always get on the end of things as he had such power in the air. In those days they did not bend free kicks – but if there was a gap in a wall he would power it through.

'When I came back from London in 1953 I played for Tom in Pwllheli up to the end of the 1953/54 season. You have never seen a more vain man in all your life. He was a sun-worshipper with physique – he was like a country gent and he would wander down the Lleyn Peninsula on these lovely beaches. But he was a great, great centre-half – there are no two ways about it. Dixie Dean had seen John Charles at his best and was no fool – he knew football and was adamant that T.G. was the greatest, most complete player seen.'

Roberts recalls that, although troubled by his long-standing ankle complaint, T.G. was far from finished as a footballer: 'Some may have said that his ankles had gone, and he did have agricultural-type football boots to protect them, but he looked after himself – he was a fit lad and not a heavy drinker. Imagine having played at Anfield and Highbury, and he was now playing on bloomin' cow-pat pitches in most instances. In those years he wasn't extended except on occasions when he met the likes of Don Spendlove of Rhyl or Tommy Welsh of Holyhead. At the Rec we had a bit of a walk from the changing room to the field and, as the goalkeeper, I would walk out behind Tommy. Once, we were beating some team four or five-nil at half-time. He turned round to me as we walked out and said, "I don't like these games but we'll have a good time next week against Flint."

'You never found Tommy Jones on his backside. with his balance you hardly ever found him on the floor - he'd argue that you were at a disadvantage there. One occasion where he ended up on his knees was in Pwllheli. The ball was bobbling about and I came out and bloody well gave it one. The ball went somewhere then I turned around and Tommy was on the floor. There was a pool of blood – I had hit him. He would never swear but he did that day: "That bastard goalkeeper!"'

As at Everton, where Thomson, Mercer, Cook and Greenhalgh's bite had complemented his artistry, Roberts recalls that T.G. preferred Pwllheli teammates who would act as his 'attack dogs': 'He would instil in me who were the real footballers: the Scottish wing-halves Jimmy Scoular and Tommy Docherty; and Wilf Copping, of England and Arsenal, who reportedly sorted the Italians out once. He wanted players with a bit of bite. T.G. was the artist and the show and he was sending out all the other players to "kill that fellow". It was like those film posters for Ben Hur: T.G. was riding on the chariot, and his teammates were the horses carrying him along.'

After a relatively mediocre 1952/53 season, Pwllheli were once again challenging for the title in 1953/54. As in 1950/51, it went to the wire with a glut of final-week fixtures. Victory over Bangor City reserves would have confirmed a third league championship for Pwllheli, but on a boggy pitch chances were spurned and the score ended 1–1. This still left nearest rivals RA55 Tonfanau (the artillery camp team) needing to win by five clear goals in their final fixture against Colwyn Bay. Unfortunately for Roberts and his Pwllheli teammates, Colwyn Bay, with nothing to play for, sent a scratch side featuring only ten players to fulfil the fixture held at Porthmadog's Traeth ground: 'We lost the league by a fraction of a goal – we played five matches that last week. Bangor reserves had put a strong side out against us on the Saturday night but the story went that Colwyn Bay had gone to play Tonfanau and were picking people up on the way. Tonfanau won 12–0. T.G. was so annoyed – we were sure that we had won the league.'

With T.G. obliged to field a reserve team in the Alves Cup final due to fixture congestion, the season ended trophyless, as did T.G.'s three remaining seasons at the helm. Although T.G. was the star attraction of the league, Ifor Roberts recalls vividly how his disdain for authority won him few friends: 'T.G. would bring a football to the away game and tell the referee, "That's no good; use my ball." And he would lecture referees during matches. It didn't endear him to people!'

One such referee was the Anglesey-based Gwylim Owen, who was still in his teens when T.G. arrived in Pwllheli. He had the unenviable task of officiating matches where each team supplied its own linesman: 'I have pleasant memories, if a referee can have any. It was a very closely fought league, with Pwllheli, under Tommy, the team to beat. It was always an experience with Tommy. He had a good team and believed in them and himself but he didn't have much time for referees. I never sent him off but had occasion to warn him. I never had the benefit of neutral linesmen so each team had, in effect, twelve players. You were there on your own as a referee. The club linesmen could give you hell and tried to rule the roost. Tommy used to shout at his club linesman, "Put that bloody flag up!" and then he would comply.

'Before one game at Holyhead, Pwllheli got changed in an old railway wagon and through the vent at the top I could hear Tommy give the team talk. I heard him issuing his instructions to Idris Evans: "That fellow at inside-left – get him and we'll win this game." And Idris would reply: "Yes, Tommy, I'll do it, Tommy!" I remember walking out behind Tommy as we went out onto the field, and I warned him: "I heard what you told Idris so I will be looking out. I know what will happen, Idris will be sent off and that will be the end of the game for you." He replied, "Mind your own bloody business – do you know who you are talking to?" That was always his line to me. He wasn't swearing but that was the way he liked to run his Pwllheli team.

'Tommy was in his prime – he was extremely fit. He was a brilliant player and a great character on the field. A team-builder and you had to watch him – he wasn't breaking the rules but, my God, he knew how to bend them. I remember once he wanted to see an opponent sent off. I gave the free kick but told Tommy that I was not sending the player off. Tommy replied, "He should go off for that!"

to which I replied, "It's a free kick – put the ball down and take it." He put it down but didn't try to kick it upfield. I had made the mistake of turning my back on him, and as I walked away the ball whistled past my ear – if it had hit me I'd have been dead, because of the way he hit the ball at a hundred miles an hour. That was Tommy's way of saying, "Thank you for not giving in to me."

'For Tommy, all the boys looked up to him, but us "bloomin' referees" were trying to tell him off. He clearly thought, "Who is this bum from Anglesey coming to point his finger at Tommy Jones?" Sometime later, I heard him say that I wasn't a bad referee, in his eyes, so I mustn't have sinned too much against him!'

A teenaged Tony Ensor occasionally played golf with T.G. and Hubert Hughes at Pwllheli Golf Club (T.G. was a member, playing off a single-figure handicap). He recalls that T.G., such a clean footballer in his prime, had to resort to the darker arts as age diminished his mobility and agility: 'He naturally faded, and not gracefully. I'll put it that way. He committed what we'd now call professional fouls – they didn't have yellow cards, of course.'

Ensor's observation is backed up by T.G. being sent off in a match against Caernarvon in December 1953 – seemingly for the first time in his career. He escaped significant sanction from the Welsh League, as the local press reported: 'Jones is to be cautioned as to his future conduct. The Committee took into account his long and distinguished career. One entirely free from serious misconduct.'(CDH)

Contemporary newspaper reports illustrate, vividly, how matches could easily descend into chaos. Play in a Welsh Senior Cup tie against Borough United at the Rec was stopped after a spectator 'tackled' Idris Evans – resulting in a cut to the right-back's shin. At the final whistle T.G. was struck on the neck by an apple core used as a projectile. He described to the local press how he took matters, and the apple-throwing assailant, into his own hands: 'I got hold of him and gave him a good shaking. His action was bad sportsmanship.'(CDH)

One notable non-competitive fixture was a fundraiser for the 1955 Eisteddfod in which T.G.'s Pwllheli took on a John Charles XI featuring many of the Leeds United star's teammates as well as his footballing brother, Mel. Charles, who would regularly holiday in the town, was justifiably considered to be the heir to T.G. on the national and international stage. His transfer to Juventus came two years later, no doubt rekindling T.G.'s memories of his aborted move to Roma. When asked to rate himself against Charles, in 1997, T.G. replied: 'John was a big strong lad – while he hadn't my ability to play with the ball he was bigger and stronger. Let's say we were equal in the air; his strength was out of this world.'[AS]

T.G. recalled with fondness Charles' kind words after the match: 'He came to stay with me in Pwllheli. There was a dinner with John as one of the guests. I always remember that during his speech he said something which pleased me tremendously: "I worked out my career after watching Tommy Jones." I thought it was very nice of him – whether he meant it or not.'[AS]

In the mid-1950s, Flint Town United were entering a period of domination of the Welsh League North, yet T.G. remained happy at Pwllheli as the big fish in a small pond. Indeed, looking back at his playing career in 1970, he made a remarkable claim: 'I think that I played my best football in the comparative obscurity of Pwllheli.'[EP] Maybe he genuinely believed this or perhaps the comment was a provocative one, reflecting his acrimonious departure from Everton.

T.G. could not resist the call of his former club in 1956, however, when Cliff Britton parted company with Everton in acrimonious circumstances. After their battles at Goodison in the late 1940s, one can imagine T.G. allowing himself a wry smile when Britton resigned from the managerial post over perceived interference and undermining from some board members. T.G. applied for the vacant post and found himself short-listed for interview alongside Ian Buchan (a physical education lecturer at Loughborough College), former Everton half-back Maurice Lindley, Luton Town coach Harry Wright, and former England international player George Hardwick.

To the shock of all observers, the directors appointed Ian Buchan, who, in spite of only having played amateur football in Scotland, impressed the interview panel with his plans for a more scientific approach to fitness and training. The club were seeking to dilute the power of the manager's post (the role was retitled 'Chief Coach' to reflect this). Selecting the opinionated, strong-willed T.G., who had walked away from the club a few years previously, was considered too great a risk. T.G., understandably, was livid with being passed over in favour of someone from outside the professional game. More than forty years later, the anger was still in evidence when he told David France: 'They thought that a PE teacher would be a better leader of men than "The Prince of Wales".' A year later, however, T.G. would move to fresh pastures, albeit nowhere approaching the grandeur of Goodison Park.

CITIZEN OF BANGOR

THE 1956/57 SEASON HAD BEEN CALAMITOUS FOR BANGOR City Football Club – known as the Citizens to its supporters. Player-manager Roland Depear's team finished second from bottom of the Cheshire League; only Crewe Alexandra reserves accumulated fewer points. With Depear standing down, rumours circulated that T.G. was in line for the post, but Emrys Edwards, the Bangor City chairman, did not start the recruitment process until league re-election was secured by just two votes on 17 May.

Nearly fifty applications were received for the manager's position – many from candidates plying their trade as players in the Football League. Approached for comment as to whether he would apply T.G.'s response showed typical bravado: 'I will certainly not apply for any job. If approached personally, it may be a different matter.'[CDH] It appears that it was a case of 'Muhammad must go to the mountain' as, on the evening of 4 June, Emrys Edwards, plus the club secretary and two other directors, visited the Tower Hotel to negotiate terms with T.G. The following day, a short press statement was released: 'Tommy has agreed to accept an offer, and is assured of a warm welcome at Bangor.'[CDH]

Pwllheli FC agreed to T.G.'s release and made their own statement: 'We are sorry to lose such a colourful personality. He made Pwllheli the most successful and most talked-about club in post-war football in North Wales. Naturally we could not stand in his way.' T.G., for his part, told the Caernarvon and Denbigh Herald: 'I have made my decision, although not without some regret. However, I hope to lead Bangor to the top of the Cheshire League next season.'[CDH]

For a period, T.G. would combine the role of Bangor City manager with holding the tenancy of the Tower Hotel. The timing of the Bangor City appointment was fortuitous because off-field matters in Pwllheli were coming to a head. Elis Jones explains that while T.G. enjoyed the status of having his name above the door at the Tower Hotel, he was ill-suited to the role: 'Pwllheli was booming then, chock-a-block with visitors and farmers on Wednesdays. Tommy could be seen outside the Tower. "Look, it's Tommy Jones!" they'd say. He drew them in and they bought pints and food there. But Tommy was not to be seen with the hordes – he wasn't very good with people. He would be in the back room with Orig Williams, having a cup of tea and chatting about Saturday's match.'

T.G. somewhat neglected his role at the hotel, preferring to gallivant around the region, scouting for new players, sunbathing on the beautiful beaches and indulging in other pleasures. Lacking business acumen, he failed to capitalise on the lucrative custom that his celebrity status could generate. Ifor Roberts recalls that it was left to Joyce, aided by family members like her brother, 'Big Tom' Thomas, to shoulder the burden of running the hotel: 'The business head in that marriage was undoubtedly Mrs Jones – she shouldered the main responsibility.' The strain would be detrimental to Joyce's health, while T.G.'s lack of entrepreneurial drive and discipline saw both himself and the business accumulate considerable debts. Eventually owners T.M. Jones and Dr Idris Jones had to step in and take back control of the hotel – paying off debts from their own pockets. The sour taste left by the financial troubles at the Tower Hotel would not prevent T.G. from remaining on good terms with them, however. When Dr Jones was terminally ill in 1971, his son was surprised to find T.G. on his doorstep. He had heard of Doc's condition and had come over from Bangor expressly to spend some time with him. Similarly, upon the death of T.M. Jones in 1977, his son Dafydd received a touching letter of condolence from T.G. His seven-year stay in Pwllheli is still fondly recalled by the older residents of the town. John Cowell sums up the impact that he had both on and off the pitch: 'Later generations might be doubtful of the superlatives used by those who saw him but he was a legend in his own time. North Wales football had never before seen his kind, nor is ever likely to again.'

In time, the family, which had been expanded by the birth of Elizabeth in 1952 and Jane in 1956, relocated to Tresco, a rented property in the bucolic hamlet of Pentir, located above Bangor. After the stresses of the final months in the Tower Hotel, life in Pentir was idyllic by comparison. It was here T.G. displayed what a good father he could be, and began to indulge, with unforeseen results, in his lifelong love of animals. His daughter Jane recalls: 'Dad decided that Elizabeth and I could have a rabbit each. He thought, wrongly, that they were both male, and built a nice hutch and run for them. We ended up with forty-two rabbits! So he was selling them to people – one person kept coming to buy them until he realised he was eating them and he put a stop to that! We had Cathy, the little horse that he found. Like a typical good father, he walked miles on foot with one of us riding her. Dad might have been a right bugger later on, but as children we had anything we needed – we had a good childhood.'

T.G.'s nephew, Chris Kozlowski, remembers happy times spent with his uncle and cousins: 'I found Tom to be a really nice guy. I used to travel with him, Liz and Jane and he used to tell us the names of the mountains and the folklore of the area. He used to sing little ditties as we drove along; it was most entertaining.'

T.G. joined Bangor City as a player-manager just a few months before his fortieth birthday, and found himself reunited with former Pwllheli goalkeeper Ifor Roberts. By chance, Roberts, who had signed for Bangor upon completing his national service, was passing Bangor's Farrar Road stadium as T.G. arrived outside in his station-wagon. He witnessed a scene which illustrated T.G.'s disdain for authority: 'Ron Depear would call the club chairman "Alderman" or "Mr Edwards" in a deferential manner. But Tom got out of his "shooting brake" vehicle and said, "Emrys – go in the back and get my bag out." That was the type of man that Tom was; Ron Depear would never have said that!'

T.G.'s prediction of taking Bangor to the top of the Cheshire League immediately was over-optimistic, but the first season saw a respectable eighth-place finish. The team were disappointed to go out of the Welsh Cup at the semi-final stage, losing to Wrexham. The FA Cup would take T.G. back to Merseyside as Bangor took on Prescot Cables in the second qualifying round. Prior to moving from Pwllheli to Pentir, T.G. used to collect Ifor Roberts from the goalkeeper's Caernarfon home while en route from Pwllheli to Bangor or some away fixture. Roberts recalls the journey to Prescot and how T.G. revelled in the adulation still showered on him in Merseyside: 'T.G. stopped the car in Liverpool and called this fellow over. As T.G. wound the window down, the fellow looked and exclaimed, "T.G.!" I can't recall if T.G. really wanted the directions to Prescot Cables but afterwards, as he wound the window back up, he turned to me and said, "You see, Ifor? They still remember me."' Silverware did come to Farrar Road that season when Bangor, enjoying home advantage in the final against Holyhead, won the 1958 North Wales Coast Challenge Cup.

T.G.'s path would once more cross that of another great centre-half, Neil Franklin, in the late 1950s. By this stage, Franklin, hampered by injury and age, was winding down his career at Stockport County of the Third Division North. The episode, recounted by Ifor Roberts, serves to illustrate how T.G. was protective of his status in the game: 'We had lunch in Chester before playing Stockport County reserves at Edgeley Park. Tommy was incapacitated at that time with a horrendous knee injury. On the coach, our centre-forward, Len Rowden, had the provincial newspaper and mentioned: "Oh, I'm playing against Neil Franklin today – he's the best centre-half I've ever seen." We knew that we were playing a strong County line-up that day with a lot of first-teamers in it. It was a hard-fought 1–1 draw in which Rowden had gone round Franklin like a dose of salts to score. We came off at the end very satisfied with the draw, but Tom was waiting for us in the dressing room. By God, he could lay it on, no swearing but he went about it: "Not only have you insulted Bangor City but you have insulted me." Eddie Benyon, our skipper, threw it back at him. "Tom, this is championship form: win at home and draw away." Then we all trooped into the big baths, not very happy. The next thing, Tom's face came round, looked at us in the bath, and said, "And anyway, I can think of a better centre-half than that clown." So it wasn't the result that had got to Tom – it had been Len Rowden praising Franklin – he was so vain. So we ducked Len into the water!'

T.G. started to remould the Bangor City team – drawing on his connections in the game – as he told HTV in the 1990s: 'I was very fortunate I'd been at the top of the tree and I knew everybody and everybody knew me. I would go down to see Wales play. I knew all the players and the people around football.'

His second campaign ended in a second-place finish. A final-day 3–1 victory over Ellesmere Port saw T.G. lift the Edward Case Cup, awarded to the championship runners-up. There to congratulate him was his former Everton teammate Cyril Lello, who was by now Ellesmere Port's player-manager. T.G. addressed the crowd on the pitch – thanking them for their support and apologising for some late-season slip-ups which had stymied any chance of claiming top spot. 'But that's how it is in football,' he declared to the crowd. The team would also get as far as the semi-finals of the Welsh Cup – a feat repeated the following year.

By now, age was catching up with T.G. and he stood down from regular playing duties at the end of the season. Sports journalist Keith Evans, who covered Bangor for the North Wales Chronicle and Daily Post, and who came to work closely with T.G. during his time managing City, recalls the autumn of T.G.'s playing days: 'When I saw him play for Bangor it was at the end of his career. He was struggling a bit and was under some pressure from the club to stop playing, as it was reckoned that he was becoming a bit of a liability. But his class got him by – he was just ambling around the penalty box using his experience, height, knowhow, timing and intelligence to deal with any problems.'

Eric Thomas, a Bangor supporter since the late 1930s, recalls T.G. as a player-manager: 'He was a brilliant centre-half and was really fit. He never wandered from the middle; he let all the younger players do the running whilst he sprayed passes to the left and right. His passing and free kicks were immaculate. If Bangor were losing at half-time, they'd either draw or win in the second half, so he must have given them a terrible roasting at half-time if they weren't performing. If they did lose, he'd keep the players in the changing room for a long time. Tommy was immaculately dressed and always took a long time getting changed. After an away game, the others used to have to wait for him on the coach; the coach driver used to go potty.' Thomas also recalls that T.G.'s reputation, earned at Pwllheli, for scolding match officials was bolstered at Bangor: 'He used to moan to the referees quite a lot. He had come out of the Everton team and the refs in the Cheshire League weren't as good. He was seeing all kinds of fouls and they weren't given so he was always complaining. He wasn't very popular with visiting supporters.'

Ifor Roberts recalls one incident when keeping goal for Bangor against Port Vale: 'That day we were cruising, 3–0 up, and I was looking for my clean sheet. Tommy was posing about and lost the ball, Griffiths walked the ball in for Port Vale to make it 3–1. I thought I'd be like Ted Sagar and bloody well told him off – but by the time we went home, he had convinced everybody that it was my fault!' Despite this incident, Roberts also remembers that T.G. was capable of turning back the clock and displaying flashes of genius on the pitch: 'We played at Wellington [now called Telford United] in the Cheshire League. They had the ex-Wolves goalkeeper, Dennis Parsons, playing for them. Bangor were awarded a free kick, a bit out wide. Tom would normally take free kicks a bit like Ronald Koeman – he'd spot a space and go for a ball driven with power. On this occasion, I can well remember, he came loping up to the ball. Parsons came out to narrow the angle, Tom checked at the last moment and clearly thought, "I'll put the driver away and go for the nine iron." He arrived at the ball and chipped it deftly – with Parsons rushing out, it flew over his head and into the net.'

T.G. would not give up playing completely in 1959 and would make the occasional appearance in a variety of positions for the reserves and first team, as player shortages dictated. Bangor supporter Neville Williams recalls that, although lacking in pace, T.G. turned out at right-back for the reserves, shepherding wingers away from danger areas without resorting to rash tackles. Like Ifor Roberts, Williams has likened T.G.'s kicking technique, especially from set-pieces, to a golfing iron shot, heavy leather balls notwithstanding.

As at Pwllheli, T.G. would try to use his stature to influence match officials, but not always successfully. Ifor Roberts recalls one such occasion at the turn of the decade: 'It was a club eleven match which we had to fulfil at the end of the season at Flint United. Tom was mainly playing in the reserves at this stage. The pitch was terrible – rock hard – and Tom told the referee: "There is no way we're playing on this," but referee Tom Parry ignored him. In the match Tom scored from a free kick and trotted back with his chest puffed out with pride. Tom Parry ran after him, saying, "You don't want me to call the match off now, do you, Mr Jones?"'

T.G.'s justifiable assertion that he had been the greatest of centre-halves could come across as arrogance to some. He would bristle if other centre-halves were compared favourably to him. In 1958, there was a pre-season Bangor City public trial match held between the nominal first and second teams (Blues and Reds) at Farrar Road. Joe Mercer, then managing Sheffield United, had come to see his old friend, and to run the rule over Bangor's Glyn Owen – an outstanding amateur international left-half who he was considering signing. Ifor Roberts recalls an exchange in the dressing room which encapsulated T.G.'s opinion of himself as a player: 'Into the dressing room comes Joe Mercer and stands next to me – my peg was number one next to the door and Tommy's was at the far end. That summer [we had been following] Wales' participation in the World Cup Finals on television. Tom was communicating with Joe across the dressing room and said, "Did you see the World Cup in Sweden, Joe? Watching that, I still think I am the best centre-half in the world." That was the vainness of the man. Joe looked at me and just smiled!'

By way of contrast, former teammate Orig Williams interviewed his erstwhile mentor for a 1997 newspaper article and sought to counter the view that T.G. had an inflated opinion of himself. Instead, he put forward that T.G. was merely not one for false modesty:

> *Throughout his career and until today the self-confidence flows from him. A fact that makes some people keep away from him. But knowing him well you realise that this is not an old act. It is self-belief by a man who believes that he was the best. This shines through his conversation with you. This frightens some of the midgets of the football world because they would be afraid that this man would laugh at their shallow knowledge of the game and would flout them. A fact that would be right.*

John Ogwen, signed at sixteen by T.G. in 1960 after being scouted playing for Bethesda School and Caernarfonshire Schoolboys, recalls: 'I liked T.G. very much. He would pick me up from home and come in and have a cup of tea and a chat with my dad – he was very pleasant. He did have a temper though – I remember he once forgot the keys for the shed where they kept the balls so he just kicked the door in. What I enjoyed most was when he took me training on my own. I came down to Farrar Road from school on the bus and Tommy would wear these black-and-white baseball boots. He was so accurate with the heavy ball – he could put it anywhere. He had tremendous skill from a dead ball, from fifty yards he'd place it three yards in front of me for me to then head.'

Ogwen also remembers that T.G. detested seeing talent go unfulfilled. According to him, T.G. was very taken with a schoolboy who perhaps reminded him of himself. At six feet tall and able to play any position, T.G. regarded this particular local schoolboy as one of the greatest prospects he had seen. However, when he had called by one lunchtime en route from training, he discovered that the lad was still in bed. 'Tell him to stay there,' T.G. had told the teenager's aunt. 'If a sixteen-year-old is still in bed at midday, then I don't want to know.' There was nothing to overcome T.G.'s anger at the perceived squandering of talent, and the lad never played for Bangor again.

Barry Jones was a teenager at the time of T.G.'s arrival at Bangor and remembers the impact made by his distant relation: "I lived at 24 Farrar Road, immediately behind the stadium. My first memory of the changes Great-Uncle Tommy brought to Farrar Road was the music played over the public address system. Dirge-like music, by today's standards, used to be played before matches. Tommy wanted something brighter, so, at his insistence, they started putting on a couple of Sousa's marches. The first time they played them, as I was in my bedroom getting ready for the match, it was a hell of a racket and I thought, "That's different." One, the "Liberty Bell", later became famous as the Monty Python theme – you can imagine supporters marching onto the terraces to that. Then they would turn the record over and play the other side. It was always the same two tunes come rain, hail or sunshine.'

9

NAPOLI

AFTER SLIPPING BACK TO A SEVENTH-PLACE FINISH IN THE
1959/60 season, T.G. made some key close-season signings in anticipation of the
next campaign. His philosophy was summed up in an interview given to HTV
in the late 1990s: 'When I came to Bangor I went out to get a top-class team.
When you build a football team you have to have first of all supreme strength
in the middle. If you've got that you can start on the rest but you must get
that first.' This point is echoed by Roy Matthews, a one-time Manchester City
youth winger, recruited by T.G. from Winsford in 1961. He recounts how T.G.
structured his teams: 'Tommy based his sides in the same way as Brian Clough.
He always wanted an outstanding goalkeeper, a very dominant centre-half and a
centre-forward that could head them in from any angle. It was all about getting
forward – we daren't pass the ball backwards.'

T.G.'s tactics and training regimes were not sophisticated and would have
borne close resemblance to those adopted by T.G. and his fellow players at
Goodison Park two decades earlier. Physicality in the spine of the team was

demanded. Roy Matthews records an exchange between T.G. and Eddie Murphy, the former Oldham Athletic centre-half recruited from Tranmere Rovers: 'Once we were getting beaten 2–1 at half-time and Tommy turned to Eddie and said: "Eddie! For Christ's sake, their centre-forward has scored two. You're the centre-half – next time he comes near you give him what I refer to as the Bangor tackle. Eddie asked what that was, to which Tommy replied: "Anywhere beneath the bloody chin."'

Former Everton and Southampton wing-half Ken Birch joined from Chelmsford as club captain, and ex-Burnley full-back Bill Souter made the short journey from Chester. In the autumn, they would be joined by former Arsenal centre-forward Eddie Brown. T.G. returned to Merseyside to secure the £500 acquisition of Liverpool's half-back, Barry Wilkinson, and later recalled: 'Barry Wilkinson had got in the Liverpool first team but got into trouble with Bill Shankly and Bill let me have him.'[AS] He would elaborate on this during an HTV interview: 'Barry had gone to play in South Africa during the summer and Bill Shankly, Liverpool's new manager, was livid and said that he would never kick a ball in football again. I had heard of this and persuaded Shankly, an old friend, to let me sign Barry for Bangor. I met him off a banana boat and he signed. He could have played for England, he was that good.'

About the rest of the half-back line he added: 'I got to know about Eddie Murphy, an under- 21 Scottish international with Oldham. I told him he was better off with me than at Oldham. I got him a job and a house and decent wages.'[HTV]

About his new captain, he was to say: 'Ken Birch was a former Everton player who, the year before he came to me, had been captain of Southampton. Don't ask me how I got them. I don't know really! I was surprised when they signed for a non-league club but they were terrific players.'[AS]

When signing players in the autumn of their careers, T.G. would hoodwink club directors and the press about their true ages. Programme notes would invariably describe players as being in their mid-to-late twenties when, in fact, they were the wrong side of thirty. When challenged by local journalists about the veracity of the quoted ages, T.G. had responded, with a twinkle in his eye: 'I never sign anyone over twenty-nine.' With the abolition of the Football League's maximum wage cap in 1962, clubs were obliged to trim their bloated squads in order to balance the books. Non-league clubs benefitted by picking up many of the released players. As well as offering competitive wages, Bangor enticed part-time professionals with offers of accommodation in the city and employment at local workplaces. The nearby Ferranti works was a favoured employer for players because club directors held positions there, but others were considered. For example, goalkeeper Graham Griffiths was fixed up with a car sales position on Anglesey when he declined a position at Ferranti. Other players chose to remain living across the border near Manchester and Liverpool, commuting over on match days.

Jim Conde, who joined the club in 1966, recalls how he, like numerous others, was tempted to swap Merseyside for North Wales: 'I was full-time at Tranmere and Tommy saw me playing for the reserves in the Cheshire League. We went down to Bangor for a long weekend. It was a long way from home but Tommy sold it to us. He showed us around and took us to this beach on Anglesey at Aberffraw. We drove down this country lane through sand dunes and he said, "This is where I go in the mornings two to three times a week." The sun was shining, the sea was blue and the sand was white; it was just amazing – so we decided to move. He got us a furnished flat just across the road [from his house in Bangor]. We sat in this bay window looking over to Anglesey and it was amazing.'

In spite of T.G.'s marital peccadilloes over the years, it is clear that he and Joyce worked well as a team. When Jim Conde moved to Bangor with his future wife, Diane, T.G. and Joyce came round to their flat with some essential grocer-ies. When Joyce learned that the flat lacked pillows, she returned later with four of them. She also helped Diane settle in the city by introducing her to the local shops. These simple acts of hospitality and kindness made a lasting impression on the young couple.

Tony Broadhead was plying his footballing trade with Cheshire League rivals Oswestry Town in 1964, when T.G. launched a charm offensive to bring him to Bangor: 'I was seventeen or eighteen years old, from Speke in Liverpool. I didn't even know where Bangor was, but moving away was the best thing I ever did. Bangor were in the Welsh Cup final against Cardiff and were flying there from Liverpool Airport. Tommy invited me along to the match to meet my future teammates. Then I signed in the summer and loved the place. Tommy got me a job at the Ferranti factory – a couple of directors on the board were managers there. They were the best years of my life.'

His approach of giving his players the initiative was a reflection of his own experiences as a pre-war player at Everton: 'I don't care much for the word "coaching". There are far too many teams playing what I call "tactical football". I prefer watching players play and telling them quietly what I think – what could improve their game. If they are doing something wrong or something right – tell them quietly. Get the team together before a match, talk to them, tell them what you want. But the tactical side of the game, I haven't got a lot of time for.'[AS]

Roy Matthews concurs with T.G.'s own assessment: 'What Tommy Jones achieved with a bunch of part-timers was quite outstanding. It is testimony to his motivational skills and presence that the only had the team together for approximately one hour before every home game in which to get his message across.'

Jim Conde sheds further light on the understated approach to coaching which, he believes, moulded him into a clever forward: 'Tommy was a wonderful man who was inspiring when you listened to him. He was very confident and sure of himself, but not in a nasty way. He just loved football. He was a very good coach without realising it. Tommy would take training twice a week with Len Davies as trainer. He always got us match-fit – you did a lot of running, which was important as the Cheshire League was a hell of a good, competitive one. He used to talk to me about centre-halves and what they didn't like. He wouldn't say to me, "This is what I want you to do." Instead, he would say to me, "In this situation, as a centre-half, I would not like you doing that." He was not telling you what to do; he was telling me what the opponents didn't like. It was making me think about it – he was very clever at that.'

Tony Broadhead, whose grandson Nathan would go on to join Everton, re-calls the impact T.G. had on him as a footballer: 'He just wanted you to win. He wasn't a great tactician – it was a case of: "Just get out there, keep things simple, do your best and win." He'd just say to me, "Pick up the ball and run at people." He'd always come to you if you played well and say, "You did well today." And as a player that picks you up. In training Tommy had this ball hanging from the roof – he'd lift it up to have you stretching and jumping higher – simple things like that were effective and improved my heading. Tommy was a great man – he made me as a player and a man and I thought the world of him. I saw him near the end of his life – I was cycling near Bangor Pier and he was there walking. I said, "Hiya, Tom," and I thanked him as he made my life – that was the last time I saw him.'

The 1960/61 season was focused on cup competitions. Having dispatched Welsh rivals Wrexham in the first round proper of the FA Cup (after coming through four qualifying rounds), Bangor were given a home draw against Third Division Southport. A creditable draw was followed by a 3–1 defeat in the replay at Haig Avenue. In the Welsh Cup, Bangor progressed to the final, knocking out Football League opposition in Chester and Wrexham along the way. The final, against Swansea Town of the Second Division, was to be held midweek in Cardiff; this posed issues as most players had full-time employment. Mindful of the time-consuming road or rail journey involved in getting to the capital, Bangor chartered an airliner (as they also would in 1964) to make a day trip from Liverpool to Cardiff and back. Sadly, after taking an early lead, Bangor could not maintain it, and Swansea ran out 3–1 victors.

This experience served as vital preparation for the following season. A key addition to the squad was left-winger Reg Hunter, who had been a Busby Babe at Manchester United. His first memories of his new manager went back nearly a decade: 'When I was still at school I used to watch Tommy play at centre-half for Pwllheli when they came to Colwyn Bay. I remember that when he ran out he was quite a tall fellow, looking very fit and well tanned – you could tell that he liked the sun. I was playing at Wrexham after leaving Manchester United and got a bit disillusioned with being a full-time professional. Tommy came in for me to play part-time at Bangor whilst I was working at the Border Brewery in Wrexham.'

Hunter has positive recollections of his two-year sojourn under T.G. at Farrar Road: 'I enjoyed playing at Bangor; we had some good games and it was nice to just play part-time. Tommy was very good; I used to think that he ran the team like a professional outfit – well organised compared to many non-league clubs. He did a lot of sessions at Bangor with the local lads but in the main I only saw them at weekends as I did my midweek training with the Wrexham team or on my own.

'Tommy kept in touch by phone and we'd talk about the game ahead. He liked a lot of football being played but he was quite hard. He wasn't a shouter but there were times when we did get told off for not doing it right. You talk about presence – if you were in a room and he walked in, you'd turn round and look at him. He was well known around the area and highly respected.'

Hunter's comments about the professional approach at Bangor are given credence by the handbook issued to all players joining the club. On the front cover it told new recruits:

> *You are a Bangor City FC player. All facilities at the ground are for your benefit... It should be a point of honour with you to conduct yourself in a manner which will ensure you taking the field in a perfectly balanced mental and physical condition. This enhances your own and the club's reputation.*

Ken Birch would echo Hunter's comments, noting that T.G.'s schoolmasterly approach and professionalism in training gave Bangor an advantage over their rivals in the Cheshire League. When the opposition was flagging after seventy minutes of play, Bangor's players could dig deep and make their superior fitness levels tell. In the 1961/62 season, Bangor once again advanced to the Welsh Cup Final, upsetting First Division Cardiff City in a semi-final held at the Racecourse Ground, with Eddie Brown scoring both goals for the Citizens. T.G. recalled: 'Their manager, who was an old friend, came in to see me afterwards and said: "Listen, what do you feed them on, steak and chips?" That was because we ran rings round them.'[HTV] In the final, played on the new home-and-away basis, Wrexham took a two-goal advantage into the second leg, held at Farrar Road. Bangor's 2–0 victory on the night brought the aggregate scores level and necessitated that a deciding fixture be played. Rhyl's Belle Vue Stadium was chosen as a neutral venue for the rematch on 7 May. Brian Ellis, Eddie Brown and Reg Hunter put Bangor three ahead before Ken Barnes scored a late consolation for Wrexham from the spot.

The official gate was 12,000, but many hundreds more had barged through Belle Vue's gates to get a touchline view of Bangor's first Welsh Cup victory in the twentieth century. In the post-match pandemonium of a pitch invasion it took the victors several minutes to fight their way to the stand for the presentation ceremony. Police had to remove a number of supporters from the corrugated roof of the stand due to fears of it collapsing. The ornate trophy would have a novel use on the coach journey back from the match. A pub landlord had agreed a wager with Ken Birch that if Bangor overcame Wrexham, the bookies' favourites, he would fill the trophy with whisky. Birch persuaded T.G. to approve the detour to the hostelry to claim the bounty. When the team coach reached Bangor a crowd had gathered to cheer as it crawled along the high street to be met at the town hall by the mayor, Alderman Pritchard, alongside club chairman and mayor-elect Emrys Edwards. It was reported that Tommy Jones was almost bursting with pride. Smiling joyfully, he said: 'I've never been happier.'

Enticingly, the Welsh Cup victory brought a first taste of European football to the city. The first-round draw for the European Cup Winners' Cup was unkind on Bangor but also mouth-watering as AC Napoli, who had won the Coppa Italia, were drawn out of the hat to face the Welshmen over two legs. For Napoli, league title success would not come until the Maradona era of the 1980s, nevertheless, it was one of the most fervently supported teams in Italy and dwarfed the Cheshire League's Bangor in status and size. The club was bankrolled by Achille Lauro, an influential shipbuilding magnate dubbed il Comandante – 'The Commander'. The Napoli team which had been assembled included the Argentine-born inside-forward Humberto Rosa, a £75,000 acquisition from Juventus. Lauro had also made bold, but unsuccessful, bids to entice British exports John Charles and Gerry Hitchens from Juventus and Internazionale respectively. T.G. would attest to the vast gulf in stature between the clubs when speaking in 1994: 'We were not expected to live with the Italians. We were a collection of part-timers; the soccer world expected us to be buried under an avalanche of goals.'[NWC]

Determined that this would not be the case, T.G. went on a scouting mission. 'I didn't know anything about Napoli so I decided to go and watch them play. I didn't tell anyone at Bangor and paid for the trip out of my own pocket. When I was there I was recognised by the Napoli people, who were pleased to see me and looked after me very well.'[DP] The more cynical might speculate that the expedition also represented a golden opportunity for T.G. to indulge in his love of sunbathing. One wonders whether, during his stay, his thoughts drifted to his aborted transfer to Italy fifteen years earlier, and he pondered, 'What if?' It was reported that T.G. was further aided in his preparation by phone conversations with John Charles and Denis Law, both of whom had played against Napoli. A Bangor City supporter, living in Snowdonia, also produced (unprompted) a dossier for T.G., having written off to Italy, seeking information about the upcoming opponents.

The David and Goliath nature of the tie attracted media attention. HTV Wales filmed a documentary in the city during the build-up to the match, which included an interview with the manager. Some of it is transcribed below:

> *Q: Do you find it frustrating managing a little team of part-timers?*
>
> *T.G.: Not really, on the contrary, I think it's very interesting, more so than spending all my time with professional foot-ballers. So much more to do. We have to look after our chaps. They work and it can be awkward to get them training. Not always sure of getting them to play in midweek. Only time we can be positive of seeing them is Saturdays.*
>
> *Q: Do you honestly think you stand a chance?*
>
> *T.G.: With that sort of team we always stand a chance. We are recognised as a very strong side on our own ground.*
>
> *Q: Do you know the type of game Napoli play?*
>
> *T.G.: Vaguely. Have reports but nothing definite.*
>
> *Q: What type of tactics will you use?*
>
> *T.G. (smiling): We only have one type. We play hard.*

To aid fitness, the squad members, many of whom struggled to travel regularly to Bangor for training sessions, were afforded the use of facilities at the likes of Everton, Wrexham, Tranmere and Chester. On the Saturday before the first encounter with Napoli, T.G. fielded a weakened side in a league fixture in order to rest his first-teamers. He paid the £50 fine, imposed by the Cheshire League, out of his own pocket.

Arriving via Liverpool Airport the evening before the match, with no opportunity to train on the Farrar Road pitch, the Italians checked into Bangor's Castle Hotel, where they, reportedly, declined the chef's offer of spaghetti in favour of traditional British fayre of chip, ham, egg and soup! Interpreting duties during the stay were provided by Vittorio, a native of Naples who was employed as head waiter at the British Hotel in Bangor.

When the draw was made Wrexham FC's secretary approached Bangor with an offer to stage the tie at the larger Racecourse Ground. Wisely Bangor City's chairman, Emrys Edwards, declined the offer – relying on the home advantage given by the confines of Farrar Road. With travel costs to cover for the away leg, Edwards raised admission prices for the match, much to the chagrin of many supporters. The one pound and ten shillings (£1.50, probably the equivalent of £30 today) fee charged for a seat, or ten shillings to stand, saw to it that the ground did not reach its capacity of 14,000. The 9,000 that did come through the turnstiles – and film images suggest more snuck in – were treated to Bangor's match of the century. Lining up for the Citizens on Wednesday 5 September 1962 were:

> **Len Davies:** *A former Stoke City goalkeeper who was employed at the nearby Ferranti works. Aged twenty-seven.*

> **Bill Souter:** *Dundee-born full-back who had played for Burnley and Chester prior to his Bangor move. A mason by trade.*

> **Iorys Griffiths:** *This locally raised full-back was the only native Welsh-speaker in the team. He was on the playing staff for fourteen years. A television engineer.*

Ken Birch (captain): *Wirral-born half-back who had played full-time professional football for Everton and Southampton. Away from football, he was the caretaker of a thirteen-storey block of flats in Birkenhead.*

Eddie Murphy: *Govan-born centre-half signed from Oldham Athletic. Like Len Davies, he worked at Ferranti.*

Barry Wilkinson: *Liverpudlian left-half who had plied his trade at Anfield. His occupation was described as a 'company director'.*

Roy Matthews: *Former Manchester City, Altrincham and Winsford United right-winger. A sales representative for Crosse and Blackwell.*

Brian Ellis: *An amateur inside-right from Merseyside.*

Eddie Brown: *This centre-forward had once been on Arsenal and Chesterfield's books. Like Roy Matthews, he joined Bangor from Winsford United. A schoolmaster by profession.*

Jimmy McAllister: *A Glaswegian who had enjoyed a peripatetic career at the likes of Millwall, Greenock Morton and Bradford Park Avenue. He worked at Ferranti.*

Reg Hunter: *The Colwyn Bay-born left-winger had a first-team appearance for Manchester United to his name. He was, in 1962, studying accountancy and working at Wrexham's Border Brewery.*

Although sympathetic employers gave most players two days off work, Reg Hunter was obliged to work late into the night before the match in order to get the brewery's accounting books in order. This late finish earned him the following day off work – in time to attend T.G.'s pre-match summit, which was held at what the press described as 'a secret hotel location in Rhyl'. Having met for lunch the players had a team-talk and a stroll along the promenade. Interviewed on the eve of the big match, T.G. gave his team of underdogs a public vote of confidence while also seeking to take some pressure off them: 'Nothing worries them. Put them out against Spurs and they wouldn't be disturbed a bit. Not that we're a great side – just a bunch of healthy strapping lads who go out to enjoy their game of football. I am certainly not going round saying we'll win; it's bound to be tough and, honestly, I just don't know.'

T.G. later told the journalist Keith Evans how he had psyched up his players with kick-off approaching: 'We had such a great bunch of players and I would get them so hyped up before the match that they believed they were the equals of anyone. We set out to frighten the opposition and I convinced them that they were a goal up even before the game had started.'(DP) The last words T.G. spoke to the team in the dressing room are still seared in the memory of Roy Matthews: 'You are not only playing for Bangor City – tonight you are also representing Wales!'

Shortly before the 6.15 p.m. kick-off time, captains Ken Birch and Pierluigi Ronzon led their teams onto the pitch and exchanged pennants. Bangor had been obliged to switch into change colours of red and white in order to avoid a clash with Napoli's blue shirts. Although the visitors had the better of the early exchanges, hitting the crossbar with one attempt on goal, Bangor dragged themselves back into contention. John Ogwen watched events unfold from a mound of earth adjacent to the main stand: 'Looking back, little things stick in your mind, like how suntanned and healthy-looking the Italians were, whereas all the Bangor boys were as white as sheets. There was a guy called Amos Mariani who was the Italian national team's outside-right at the time. He was tackled by Iorys Griffiths in the first few minutes – a fair tackle – and never came near him for the rest of the match! Napoli were a better side technically, but I think that they were overawed by the crowd being so close to them and I think they underestimated Bangor.' Not only did Napoli's players have to come to terms with the close proximity of supporters to the touchline, but also with the pitch itself, which sloped from touchline to touchline and from goal-line to goal-line.

Two minutes before half-time came the breakthrough. The teenage winger Roy Matthews received a low Barry Wilkinson cross from the left flank. Having turned inside the full-back, he fired a low drive past the left hand of Pontel, the Napoli goalkeeper. Supporters flooded onto the pitch in celebration, mobbing the players in the centre circle. Police struggled for several minutes to restore order. Dutch referee Johan Martens had a message put out over the public address system warning of the abandonment of the tie should the fans not get off – and stay off – the pitch. With the team buzzing during the interval, they were treated to an appearance from the captain of Tottenham Hotspur and Northern Ireland, who was at the match on a journalistic assignment. T.G. recalled to the North Wales Chronicle: 'Danny Blanchflower came into the dressing room at half-time and I let him give the lads a pep talk. Not that it was needed; we were on top of the world.' Reg Hunter, in the dressing room during the break, recalls a slightly franker exchange between T.G. and the Northern Irish star: 'Danny Blanchflower started giving a team talk but Tommy said, "Hey, stop that! I'm the manager; you get out, now!" and he sent him out.'

In the second period, having matched Napoli, Bangor were awarded an 83rd-minute penalty when Eddie Brown was adjudged to have been impeded while tussling for a high ball. Once the vehement Napoli protests ebbed away, Ken Birch calmly strode forward and dispatched the ball into the net with aplomb. Bangor even went close adding a third when Ellis and Matthews spurned chances in the dying moments. As soon as the full-time whistle blew, the police were powerless to prevent the fans from invading the pitch once more, enveloping the local heroes. Afterwards, in spite of the half-time tongue-lashing from T.G., Blanchflower was welcomed back into the home changing room to join in the celebrations.

With the crowd chanting his name outside, T.G. told the Chronicle: 'Never in my life have I ever forecast that Bangor will win, but they did so all the same. I am immensely proud of them tonight, because not only did they win, but they won deservedly.' The Italians were gracious in defeat, and Amos Mariani declared: 'We have never experienced anything like this before. In Italy, when the spectators come onto the pitch, they do it to attack you. Here they do it to congratulate you. It didn't affect us – Bangor played very well.'

So, how did a non-league Welsh team upset the wealthy Italians? It is sometimes overlooked that, in contrast to Bangor, the visitors had yet to get their league programme underway and were, perhaps, under-cooked. Furthermore, although a part-time outfit, the majority of the hosts had vital Football League experience, in some cases in the higher echelons. T.G. had his own theories: 'The Italians couldn't understand it really – a team that played only three at the back, three in the middle, and a forward line of five players with terrifically fast wingers and a centre-forward that would go through a stone wall. I think that's how we destroyed them. We were a gutsy side and I don't think the Italian side liked that much; but don't make the mistake that they couldn't play football – these chaps could play. I know that they had just signed a centre-forward for an enormous amount of money from abroad. But I had a centre-half [Eddie Murphy] playing against him who'd been a Scottish Under-21 international, and he hardly gave him a kick of the ball. I had a great half-back line – it was the strength of the team.'[AS]

Eric Thomas, who was in the fervent home crowd that evening, believes that much of the credit deserved to go to T.G. 'When they beat Napoli it was all Tommy's planning; he had them all well drilled. He realised after ten minutes of the match that Napoli didn't like playing in Bangor's small, tight ground – they were used to a massive stadium. Tommy made the lads go full-out, as if they were playing in their own league. "Forget you're playing Napoli – just go out to win this game!" was his policy. I think that they were frightened of Bangor in the end. I have never been to a better game.'

The result caught the public's imagination in the UK and far beyond. Back pages of national dailies proclaimed the shock scoreline. Queues formed at Bangor's Plaza Cinema to see the local heroes featured in newsreel footage of the match, while viewers in the Granada region were able to watch highlights on television two days after the match. The players themselves were each awarded a £25 bonus, funded by a consortium of local sponsors. A Starways airliner was chartered to fly the fourteen-man squad and club officials to Italy a day before the second leg. Before departing from Liverpool Airport, T.G. was presented with a blue and white decorated horseshoe by city councillor E.G. Griffiths, who had found the good-luck symbol buried near his smithy. In addition to those lucky few travelling by air, approximately one hundred supporters made the long trek by road and sea to the cavernous Stadio San Paolo in order to see if the Welsh minnows could hang on to their two-goal advantage.

Upon landing in Naples T.G. laid down ground rules to mitigate against illness – Italian food, fruit and tap water were strictly off limits. T.G., when asked by the Daily Mirror's Derek Wallis whether Bangor's first-leg two-goal cushion was enough to secure victory, responded: 'No, I feel we've got to score more goals. I think that it is a good thing that there is optimism about our chances, but we must remember that we built our lead under our conditions.'

After Ken Birch passed a late fitness test on a calf-muscle injury, Bangor's line-up was unchanged from the first leg as they entered the field of play. Reg Hunter recalls his impressions of the setting: 'When we went to Napoli it was a massive stadium; I think there were maybe twenty thousand to thirty thousand inside, but it held eighty thousand so it didn't feel many. It was an awful pitch, though, uneven with longish grass.' Prior to the game, T.G. delivered a team talk described by Bill Fryer of the Daily Express as 'One of the most masterly and inspiring pre-match speeches to players that I have ever heard.'

After a goalless first half, T.G.'s pre-match prediction that his team would need to score again proved correct as Napoli wiped out the Welsh team's advantage through two second-half goals, only for Jimmy McAllister's 71st-minute riposte to put Bangor in front again. Seat cushions rained down on the pitch from frustrated Neapolitans whilst the 100-odd Bangor fans belted out a rendition of Sospan Fach. With just six minutes remaining, the increasingly desperate Napoli team levelled the aggregate score at 3–3 though Giovanni Farnello. Such was the impression made by Bangor on the home team's officials that discreet enquiries were made with a view to signing Ken Birch and Barry Wilkinson – the transfer fee sought would ultimately prove to be an insurmountable stumbling block. Had the away-goals rule been introduced three years earlier than it was, Bangor would have progressed to the next round. Instead a play-off was required. In tense negotiations between the clubs and UEFA representatives, the Napoli secretary, Enrico Zuppardi, offered to bring his team to London but only if cash-strapped Bangor could guarantee a £5,000 purse. Failing that, Lucerne in Switzerland or a West German venue were put forward as alternative venues by the Italians – these would have necessitated Bangor borrowing funds to cover the travel costs.

The proposal of a lucrative friendly against Torino had to be declined as

Bangor had a league fixture to fulfil against Buxton on the following Saturday. T.G. sought to pull in favours to secure a venue. He told the Daily Express: 'We have no money left but I consider it a wonderful opportunity to enhance British sport by appealing to the British public to attend the match. I will see Billy Wright when I get back…' Ultimately, a phone call by T.G. from Italy to Highbury helped to secure the use of the North London stadium. Twenty-two thousand supporters attended, with many making the trip from North Wales by a specially chartered train.

The match, played on a foggy London night, was another tight affair. Humberto Rosa put Napoli ahead, but Jimmy McAllister equalised and the match was deadlocked as the final five minutes approached. Bangor goalkeeper Len Davies parried a Napoli shot, Bill Souter cleared the follow-up effort off the line, but he was helpless to prevent Rosa from scoring his second goal of the game. Having secured their progression in the competition, the Italians fell at the quarter-final stage with Tottenham Hotspur going on to lift the trophy. T.G. later told Tony Coates in the North Wales Chronicle: 'I have long forgotten many experiences of my career but that day was really something special – it produced a miracle. What we achieved had never been done before – a little club keeping company in the big time – and I received letters from all round the world.' More than fifty years on, the city of Bangor has not forgotten those magical nights in North Wales, Naples and London. T.G. considered it the zenith of his career in the sport: 'They are probably the finest memories of all my time in football, and that includes at Everton.'[AS] He elaborated when interviewed, years later, by HTV: 'It was a terrific moment. In all the games I've played in and been to, this was the greatest thing I'd seen. I had spent fourteen years with Everton, was captain of Everton and Wales, but quite frankly I'd never seen anything like this. It was very special indeed and it put Bangor on the map. People ringing from all over and letters came from all over the world.'

Meanwhile, on Merseyside, Everton, the club which had been on a downward spiral when T.G. left in 1950, had been revitalised by the injection of John Moores' business acumen and his Littlewoods-backed funding. T.G.'s former teammate, Harry Catterick, had steered the club to the 1962/63 league championship in his second full season at the helm. When a celebratory dinner was held at the Adelphi Hotel in Liverpool the following September, T.G. and other members of the 1939 title-winning side were invited to attend. T.G.'s response to Catterick was an emphatic 'No'. Still smarting from being overlooked by the Everton board in 1956, T.G. went as far as to tell the club not to bother asking him to future events.

During T.G.'s decade at Bangor City, he was occasionally linked with other job vacancies. Keith Evans recalls, 'He was often associated with, or associated himself with, managerial vacancies in the Football League at nearby Chester, Wrexham and Tranmere. I suspected that he linked himself with those vacancies because he felt that's where he should be – back in the Football League.' It is a moot point as to whether T.G. lacked the ambition to move on from the city in which he enjoyed an elevated status. It is conceivable that he engineered, or at least nurtured, links in the media to other clubs' vacancies in order to bolster his bargaining position in contract negotiations with the Bangor City board. This theory is lent credence by events six weeks after the Napoli adventure. With his stock at its highest, T.G. was invited by the Cardiff City directorate to apply for the vacant managerial position at Ninian Park. Having informed Bangor City of the approach, he met a Cardiff deputation over lunch in Hereford. Bob Whiting of the Daily Post reported that Cardiff were shocked by the salary demanded by T.G. with no amount of negotiation able bridge the gap. T.G. was subsequently quoted as saying, 'I am so content at Bangor that only a handsome offer could have tempted me to move south.'

Such was the nature of non-league football that the 1962 trophy-winning side had splintered within a year. Ken Birch moved to South Africa early in 1963 while others either moved on or stood aside due to age or injury. Thus, T.G. was faced with the task of rebuilding the team. One signing, in September 1963, was Emyr ab Iorwerth, an amateur international who was persuaded by T.G. to turn professional in swapping Porthmadog FC for Bangor.

T.G. would also continue to turn to northern English clubs for new recruits. Arriving shortly before ab Iorwerth was the veteran Tommy Banks, who had excelled for Bolton Wanderers as a tough left-back and represented England at the 1958 World Cup. After two seasons at Cheshire League Altrincham FC, he was told by the chairman (and future Manchester City supremo) Peter Swales, that he would become a reserve player-coach. With a building business to fall back on, Banks advised Swales that he was quitting the game. Days later, he answered a knock on his door in Farnworth, near Bolton, and found T.G. on the doorstep. Banks recalls: 'I saw Tommy playing just after the war – I was only fifteen or sixteen – for Everton against Bolton. He stood out; he was great in the air – bigger men couldn't beat him. He was what I call a "walking pro". In my eyes, he knew what he'd do. He was very good in the air and just strolling here and there, taking it off the toes and not getting a sweat up. He was a cool customer. After I left Altrincham, Tommy found out where I lived and came to my house. He said, "Would you like a game or two?" to which I replied, "Yes, I would." He explained that he was at Bangor and I thought, "That's a fair way." There were no motorways in those days – it was 106 miles, door to door.'

After some persuading from T.G., Banks agreed to join Bangor on condition that he only travelled down to Bangor on match days. He has fond memories of T.G. and his time playing on the Welsh coast: 'Tommy was a nice chap. Once, he asked me, "I'd like to get all the lads together for two or three days' pre-season training on Anglesey: can you get off work?" So I got two or three days off and I trained with him. He was good – he knew the game and didn't talk rubbish. It surprised me that he hadn't gone to a better club in the Football League but perhaps he was satisfied and got on with the Bangor board. I got on well with him. I scored eighteen goals in one season as he let me take the free kicks and penalties. "Keep it going, Tommy – it's doing us good!" he'd say. I played at left-back and wing-half – where I always fancied myself playing. He was a good sort to me. After two good seasons we agreed that was that and I retired.'

With Banks in the side, Bangor reached the 1964 Welsh Cup final with the promise of more European football should the team emerge victorious. The two-legged affair was against a Cardiff City team containing the Charles brothers, John and Mel, in addition to Welsh international striker Ivor Allchurch. In spite of being underdogs, T.G. talked up his side's chances – having the chutzpah, in the Daily Express, to compare Bangor City favourably with the leading lights of the First Division: 'Our boys are a sweet-moving team at their best. They play the sort of football that Manchester United and the rest are trying to play.' The first leg saw Bangor shock the Bluebirds with a 2–0 win – the first goal bringing about a pitch invasion. With echoes of the Napoli game in 1962, a Tannoy message warned the interlopers that the match would be abandoned if there was any repetition. The return leg at Ninian Park saw John Charles moved forward into an attacking role. The switch reaped dividends, Cardiff's victory necessitating a replay to be played in Wrexham. There was no upset this time round as Cardiff triumphed 3–1.

In the autumn of 1964, T.G. did apply for a vacancy, albeit a part-time one which could be combined with his Bangor City role. Jimmy Murphy had stood down from the Wales national team manager's post in order to focus on his Manchester United duties in support of Matt Busby. T.G. was short-listed with four other candidates, including his friend and former Wales teammate Ron Burgess. T.G. considered Burgess, who had captained the great Spurs push-and-run team of the early 1950s, and Don Dearson, to be the best Welsh half-backs he had played alongside. When the press asked T.G. about his chances of selection, he commented: 'It's certainly a job I'd like and one I know I could do. I imagine, however, that the job will go to someone actively involved in league football.' After the interviews were held in Shrewsbury, T.G.'s prediction was realised. The FAW Council selected Dave Bowen, the Northampton manager who had played for Arsenal and captained Wales at the 1958 World Cup Finals.

In 1965, the Jones family moved from Pentir down to Garth Road in Bangor, close to the pier which juts out into the Menai Straits. They purchased a terraced house from a Mr Allenby, who was retiring from running a small newspaper-cum-sweetshop from the property. For the next thirty years they would operate the business from the front room of the house. As with the Tower Hotel in Pwllheli, although T.G. was the public face of the business, it was Joyce who put in the long hours – often getting up at 5 a.m. to start selling newspapers to passing motorists in the days before the construction of the A55 (the North Wales Expressway). One reason T.G. was not inclined to spend time serving in the shop was that he would either be carrying out his managerial duties for Bangor City or be in the back room hammering away at his typewriter.

Through a friendship with Bob Whiting of the Daily Post, T.G. had been given a regular column – Tommy Jones Says – to write in the newspaper, commenting on the North Wales football scene. Journalist Keith Evans recalls his dealings with him: 'Tommy's characteristics were: tall, elegant, good-looking, educated, articulate, and aloof on occasions. He regularly gave the impression that he had been used to better things – no doubt because of his Everton and Wales background. He had a regular column for the Daily Post on Tuesdays and Fridays – maybe three hundred words with his slant on whatever topics of the day cropped up, like the previous weekend's match or new signings. Now and again he'd be gallivanting off and would ring up on the Monday and say, "I've got to go away for the day – can you do the column for me?" Talk about last minute! So I'd have to concoct something. I never got a penny for it – it was all part of the good relationship. We had a decent relationship and he gave me freedom to quote him as I liked. He'd say, "Don't bother me, lad – just put a quote in, as long as you don't make me look foolish." It made life easier for me and I never hit any problems. He was very easy-going in that sense – we never had a cross word.'

Keith Evans also hosted Sports Medley and Special Medley, Saturday evening radio programmes broadcast from the BBC studios in Bangor. T.G. was occasionally invited on as a guest but would give Evans' production team palpitations: 'Tommy lived just down the road from the studios. There would be no sign of him and the BBC staff would be panicking as they wanted him in to settle down and prepare for the thing. Then he'd just stroll in at the last minute looking very casual and nonchalant – puffing his pipe, as if to say, "What's the panic?"… [T.G.] was a bit laid back in that way; he always gave me the impression that he was a bit bigger than the job.'

MOVING ON

IN 1966, WITH NO CHESHIRE LEAGUE TITLE WIN ACHIEVED AND the glorious encounters against Napoli becoming increasingly distant memories, some Bangor supporters objected vociferously to a long-term contract being offered to T.G. The board called a meeting with the supporters' club to try to placate the fans, but it ended sourly, with T.G. walking out and advising the directors that he intended to resign. His absence from the following weekend's Cheshire League fixture against New Brighton led to speculation that he was on the verge of leaving his post. Rhyl FC were reported to have tabled a contract offer. However, a few days later T.G. committed himself to Bangor. The eventual signing of a four-year contract, with a significant salary increase, could not suppress the feeling among many supporters that T.G.'s time at Bangor was approaching its natural end.

A new era in non-league football was about to be ushered in by the unveiling of the Northern Premier League in the summer of 1967. The brainchild of Altrincham FC chairman, Peter Swales, it was intended to pave the way for the introduction of automatic promotion to, and relegation from, the Fourth Division of the Football League. In the event this particular breakthrough did not come about for two decades. Bangor City was accepted as a founder member of the new league, which was scheduled to commence in the 1968/69 season. But when Bangor got their final Cheshire League campaign under way T.G. was no longer at the tiller.

A clue that matters were reaching a head was given by newspaper reports in early July that pre-season training had begun with T.G. conspicuous by his absence. This was put down to him being away on scouting duties for potential signings. He was quoted as stating that he was having 'a great difficulty persuading them to travel, especially for mid-week games'.(NWC) Perhaps the lack of success on the pitch, and increased competition from other clubs in North Wales and the North West of England and was making Bangor a less attractive destination for part-time professionals.

Tom Cowell, a cousin of John Cowell, T.G.'s erstwhile goalkeeper at Pwllheli, joined Bangor's board early in 1967 and can recall the events leading to T.G.'s departure: 'I was only at Bangor City for a few months as a director with Tommy as manager. He could be a bit fiery at times but I got on fine with him. A Bangor fellow called Arthur Lunn had joined Bradford Park Avenue as a scout and used to come home after the game every weekend. He had rung some of the Bangor directors, including me, to tell them that Mick McGrath, the former Eire international, had been released by Bradford and was available for transfer. I said, "Look, you should tell Tommy. It's no good telling me, Arthur."

'Then there was a board meeting where Tommy felt that some of the directors were having a go at him about signing players. Tommy just got a bit fed up with this and walked out from the job.'

A year after Rhyl's unsuccessful approach to T.G., it was he who approached them this time round. After several covert meetings with Rhyl chairman Graham Roberts and director Eric MacDonald, a three-year contract was agreed. T.G.'s request to be released from his Bangor contract three years early was ratified at a board meeting on 24 July. Mick McGrath was immediately appointed as his successor. T.G. told Bob Whiting: 'Ten years is a long time. It may be that a new face and new ideas will be good for Bangor. I leave Bangor on the best of terms with everyone. My ten years there have been happy and we have achieved a great deal. Now I think a new challenge will be good for me, good for Bangor and good for Rhyl. The Rhyl job is a great challenge. I can promise nothing except hard work there.'[(DP)]

Reaction from Bangor supporters to T.G.'s departure, in letters published in the local press, was mixed. While some expressed regret, others felt ready for a change, citing a lack of development of local talent as a reason. Bangor forward Jim Conde recalls the reaction of the Bangor players to Tommy's departure: 'We were all totally bemused and shocked when he went but we didn't know the ins and outs of it all. When we used to play Rhyl, it wasn't a very nice atmosphere.'

The move was ill-starred for Tommy – crossing the Rubicon to fierce local rivals was always destined to be a difficult proposition. It would prove to be an unhappy tenure, which Ifor Roberts likened to Brian Clough swapping Derby County for Leeds United in the 1970s. According to goalkeeper Graham Griffiths, who had also swapped Bangor for Rhyl that summer, the team started the season 'like a house on fire'. However, some at the club did not take to his blunt, sometimes acerbic, way of speaking to people. This is illustrated by Roy Matthews' recollection of an incident a few years previously in the Bangor City changing room: 'A new centre-forward had come in and played seven or eight games without scoring. Pre-match, Tommy said, "Since you've been here you've played eight games and you haven't scored." The guy said, "Yes, Tommy, but I have been really unlucky. I have had two headers which hit the bar but could have easily gone in. And the other week that shot of mine hit the post but didn't go in. I know that I haven't scored but I want you to know that there is no need to worry, I will score." "I'm not worried – you've been dropped," was Tommy's deadpan response.'

With the team having only one league win since September, the Rhyl board discussed T.G.'s position at length in mid-January, amid speculation that former Everton right-back Alex Parker might replace him. He was granted a stay of execution but was controversially dismissed on 6 May 1968. Cryptically, Rhyl chairman Graham Roberts said that the sacking was based on 'quite a number of factors'. He also briefed reporters that, contrary to reports of a three-year agreement, T.G. had been employed without a contract on a week-to-week basis. 'That arrangement has now been terminated,' he added. Breaking ranks, vice-chairman Eric MacDonald went public in stating that he, and some other directors, considered the sacking a retrograde step. He noted that T.G. had accepted a salary cut to aid the club's financial position. T.G., when asked to comment on the situation, said tersely, 'The matter is in the hands of my solicitors. I have been advised at this stage to say nothing.' Upping the ante, with Rhyl's home fixture against Winsford approaching, T.G. tipped off a press photographer that he would be watching the game from the Kop as a paying spectator. A photo of T.G. among the Rhyl fans duly appeared in the local press.

After his unhappy spell at Rhyl, T.G. turned away from day-to-day involvement in football management and focused on his journalistic career. He was elevated to the role of a football correspondent for the North Wales edition of the Daily Post by Bob Whiting. This was a post in which he would take great pride, sitting in a makeshift office space in the house, hammering away on the typewriter with plumes of smoke drifting from his pipe. A limited formal education did not hold T.G. back from being an eloquent, perceptive writer. Using his extensive contacts in the North Wales football scene, he produced excellent copy in the form of match reports and pieces about what was happening across the region. Sadly, a falling-out would see him lose this coveted role in 1971.

T.G. lived in modest circumstances at the dawn of the 1970s, but his old friend and teammate Tommy Lawton was now in desperate financial straits. T.G. had lost touch with the forward in the early 1950s as he moved from Nottingham to London, upon joining first Brentford and then Arsenal. With Lawton's predicament becoming public knowledge, Joe Mercer stepped in to organise a fundraising testimonial match. The game, held in November 1972 at Goodison Park, saw an Everton XI take on a Great Britain XI featuring Bobby Moore and Bobby Charlton. The evening was the last time that a number of Everton's stars of the 1930s, including T.G., Britton, Mercer, Lawton, Sagar, Watson and Dean, would be reunited. Six years later T.G. declined, at the last moment, an invitation to see many of this former colleagues at Everton's centenary celebration dinner.

Probably looking to boost his income, T.G. was tempted back for a football swansong in January 1973, at Bethesda Athletic, a few miles up the A5 from Bangor. The role, without a formal contract, was described as that of 'team adviser' rather than a managerial appointment. This saw him return to the Welsh League North, where he had enjoyed happier times with Pwllheli. Ifor Roberts, then working in the leisure services sector, recalls stumbling across his former manager when taking in a game at Bethesda: 'It was very sad. I saw Tom coming out of the dressing room. I don't think he wanted me to see him there and he said to me: "Oh, Ifor. I've not got much to do with these people; they've just asked me to help out." He was going there for a quid or two, I suppose, but it was a pathetic situation for a man of his background. He stayed hardly any time there; it just shows how things can change.'

Dave Hughes was a player with Bethesda at this time and recalls: 'I knew Tommy from years ago, from when I played against Bangor for Wrexham reserves. Tommy had not been in football for a while so he got Ray Jones in as his main man. Tommy was only there for a season; I think he expected to do quite well but it didn't really work out. He was like a recluse then – he used to open up the shop in the morning and work for a couple of hours, then he would spend the day – winter or summer – walking on the beach on Anglesey in his sandals. He was a real character. If you were friends with him, he was OK, but he didn't take fools lightly.

'When he was at Everton he used to play it around, like the Rio Ferdinand of his era, but his Bangor City team used to kick you to death. At Bethesda, I was a centre-midfielder, and in one match we were 4–0 up in the cup and playing one-touch football. He came in at half-time and said to me, "That's not the way to play football, bang it down the middle and get your crosses in." In another game we were 2–0 down at half-time at Llandudno and he came in and said, "I've had enough of you lot, I'm going to the pictures," and he went to the cinema! He didn't come down to training much – a lad called Alan Caughter used to take it – and his pre-match talks were pretty brief. He set his standards high and thought everyone should be as good as he'd been.'

Bangor-raised John Hardy, who would become a leading broadcaster in Wales, was a teenage left-winger at Bethesda when T.G. pitched up: 'Bethesda's chairman, T.J. Jones, who owned an electricity shop on the high street, was the town's answer to Roman Abramovich and put money into the club. I was a sixteen-year-old, the only local lad in the side, and didn't know what was happening half of the time. Being a youngster, I was frightened of Tommy as manager; he was very imposing even at that age: a tall and broad man. He used to give me a lift up to Bethesda and to the away games. Before driving to a match he would meet me in the street near his newspaper shop, give me a bollocking and then say to me, "Come in and say hello to Mrs Jones." There was no doubt who the boss was: Mrs Jones!

'In the car we used to chat about games coming up, or rather, I listened. I'm an Evertonian but he never talked about his Everton days when we spent half an hour in the car before and after a match. After one game there was an Everton scout there asking me to go along for a trial, but I refused as I had my O levels coming up and was a bit insecure. Tommy had set it up but had warned the scout that I'd say no. At Bangor City it was almost as if Tommy had re-established his reputation but in later years he probably became a bit embittered with what happened. We had players coming from Liverpool, Manchester, everywhere – and we never knew if they would all turn up. I was a teenager playing amongst men. We used to do training but Tommy was never there for that.'

Shortly before the end of the 1973/74 season T.G. had severed his ties with Bethesda. When linked with a return to Bangor City he retorted: 'I treat football now as Saturday afternoon entertainment.' From then on his sole link to football was some scouting on behalf of Manchester City and, subsequently, Coventry City at the request of Joe Mercer. Sometimes T.G. would be accompanied on his scouting assignments by his friend Nigel Wright. David Wright, who often went along with his father, recalls how on one such trip T.G. spotted the potential in a young midfielder who would later become an Everton great: 'I remember T.G. saying that he had recently been to see a Bolton Wanderers junior game and how impressed he had been by a teenage midfielder by the name of Reid. This must have been ten years before Everton signed Peter.'

11

PLAYING EXTRA TIME

WITH HIS JOURNALISTIC AND FOOTBALL MANAGEMENT CAREERS at a premature end, T.G. had the newsagent's business to fall back on, although, in truth, he would duck out of the responsibilities associated with it whenever possible. He had remained in contact with several former Everton teammates during his time in Bangor, as his daughter Jane recalls: 'Dad, Joe and his wife, Norah Mercer, were extremely close friends all their lives. In fact, Elizabeth and I used to call them Uncle Joe and Auntie Norah. They frequently used to visit us in Garth, which used to cause a stir in Bangor. People came from miles around to see him and get his autograph. Quite a few footballers used to come down; Dixie Dean was one I vaguely remember.'

When on the Wirral T.G. would call in on Norman Greenhalgh, who after hanging up his football boots had become landlord at the Winslow, opposite Goodison Park, before switching to the Bromborough Hotel. Closer to home, George Milligan, an Everton teammate in the 1939/40 season, ran a holiday caravan park in North Wales and had served on the board at Rhyl FC. Milligan would remain close with T.G., with George's daughter 'Janet' knowing him as 'Uncle Tommy'. Former teammates from Pwllheli and Bangor would call in at the newspaper shop, and those he was closest to were invited into the back room for a cup of tea and a chat about football.

Although well known by local residents, T.G. kept a relatively low profile during these years of semi-retirement and was wary of people he didn't know. Glenis Pearce, daughter of the former Bangor City chairman Emrys Edwards, recalls: 'He did take a bit of getting to know but once he trusted you Tommy was warm and friendly. He had a very good heart and a dry sense of humour – but didn't suffer fools gladly.' Jane Bernad was a student in Bangor in the late 1980s when she chanced upon the man her grandfather, T.M. Jones, had enticed from Everton to Pwllheli: 'I had gone into a key-cutting shop in Bangor to get something engraved. Tommy was in there minding the shop for somebody that he knew; he was sat down and I didn't realise who he was. Next to his shoulder there was a small framed newspaper cutting on the wall about Tommy Jones and it caught my eye. I said, "That's Tommy Jones, the famous Everton football player," and there was a bit of a grunt from him. Then I said to him that it was my grandfather who had brought Tommy Jones to Pwllheli, and he said, "Oh, that was me."

'We chatted a little bit, but he wasn't very enthusiastic and didn't want to be drawn. But I did get a bit of a conversation out of him. He said that it was all a lifetime ago, so I asked if it felt like it was somebody else, and he said, "No, I've still got the aches and pains in the morning so I know it was me."'

In spite of his attractiveness to many women, T.G. was not a natural conversationalist with them, preferring male company to chew the fat with. John Ogwen recalls: 'I can't say that I knew him very well but I did spend some time in his company. I really liked him. I used to call at the shop and we'd sit down and talk – not so much about football, to be honest, but everything else. I tried a couple of times to talk about Everton with him but got nowhere! I remember one day I saw him and his wife shopping in the supermarket. Tommy and I went for a coffee and he completely forgot that she was shopping – we sat for an hour and she'd been looking for him everywhere!'

T.G. was never really gregarious, sometimes seeming to prefer the company of pets. He enjoyed walking the family dogs on Bangor Pier (ignoring the canine ban there) and up to Roman Camp, a rugged area above the city centre; if the weather was favourable, he would indulge in a spot of sunbathing. His other cherished spot was Ynys Llanddwyn, a small tidal island off the west coast of Anglesey.

His love of the sun would take T.G. abroad to far-flung places in search of warm waters to swim in and solar rays to absorb. Money earned at the newsagent's shop would be siphoned into the holiday fund rather than placed safely in the retirement pot. Joyce would not join him on these holidays; instead, he travelled alone or with his eldest daughter, Elizabeth. In light of his antiquated views on other ethnic groups, he would be teased by Joyce for returning from these jaunts 'as brown as a nut'.

Retaining the fitness and appearance of a man many years his junior, the wearing of a sizeable hearing aid was one of the few clues to his advancing years. His daughter Jane recalls: 'Dad kept his fitness practically right through until he developed dementia. Most days he walked two or three miles. He was up early at seven a.m. and swam, religiously, at Bangor pool every single morning unless he was ill. When he was younger he used to swim across the harbour to Port Penrhyn very often.'

T.G.'s nephew, Chris Kozlowski, recounts a story, possibly apocryphal, about those days of alfresco bathing: 'In the summer he used to go for a regular swim in the Menai Straits. After one such swim, he was walking home. As there was a crowd and a helicopter above, he asked what was going on. The reply was, "Oh, T.G. Jones went for a swim some time ago and has not returned. They are looking for him."'

In some ways, T.G. refused to grow old. For many years his pride and joy was a bright-green Triumph Spitfire. As he motored around North Wales he enjoyed turning heads – especially female ones. With the Spitfire becoming increasingly unreliable, T.G. took to borrowing his daughter Jane's new Ford Fiesta and passing it off to friends as his own. Jane recalls: 'I used to tell him he could borrow the Fiesta if he did not smoke his pipe while driving it. He would deny smoking, not realising I could smell it as soon as I got into the car. Eventually I had to ban him from driving it, as the smell of tobacco was unbearable. Then he would wait for me to have a lie-in, and take the car to the cash and carry. When I challenged him he would point-blank deny driving it, not realising he gave the game away by leaving the stench of tobacco behind.'

Ignoring the advice of a garage that the Spitfire was becoming a safety liability,

T.G. continued to use it. It finally met its end when the steering wheel virtually came off in Jane's hands as she turned a corner in Coed Mawr, on the outskirts of Bangor. The car was taken to the garage and left there on Jane's strict instructions that T.G. must not get his hands on it again.

The last time T.G. attended a football match was in the mid-1980s. For the first time since 1962, Bangor had qualified for the European Cup Winners' Cup and reached the second round before falling to Spanish opposition. He confessed that it left him cold: 'My ideals in soccer are vastly different from those in the modern game. The last time I watched a match was the game against Atletico Madrid in 1985 at Farrar Road. The Spaniards killed it after going two up.'(DP) He made a similar observation in a 1990 Everton programme feature: 'I think there is too much coaching in the modern game and it shows.'

In 1997, he commented ruefully on the over-complication of modern tactics, contrasting it to the methodologies of the 1930s: 'These modern tactics seem to keep the ball centred around the middle of the field most of the time, whereas we always agreed to let them have the middle of the field. The important parts to us were the two penalty boxes where you score a goal and stop a goal. The centre of the field, you can't score from there.

'They say that the game is much quicker now, but no one could be any fitter than we [Everton] were. I was very, very fit and I don't think many players today could be fitter or quicker than I was. So, the conclusion I came to is that in my day we made the ball do the work. We didn't run around like the clappers, as they do now, and end up in a tussle, almost like a wrestling match in the middle of the field. We never did that – the ball had to do the work. We'd get the ball and you always gave it to the man who called for it to you. And then you moved away and he said, "Right," and then you'd get it back.'(AS)

He also opined: 'Football has become a profession now; the money has made me green with envy. You are a millionaire in your mid-twenties, or before. When I left Everton my top wage was twelve pounds a week and you couldn't buy a lot with that. But money didn't matter, you know. That was a good wage in those days when the average was three pounds a week – but your career was so short. I think I have lost faith in the game. I've become too critical. I watch the game on TV and think, "You should not have done that." Then I think to myself – would I have done any better if I were there? I was watching Newcastle versus Barcelona on TV the other night and only watched half of it. I often do. If there is a good film on another channel, I turn over.'(AS)

Although in his later years he would feign a lack of interest in the sport, his actions did not always back this up, as Jane Jones recalls: 'He always used to say that he wasn't interested in football any more as it was "all bloody different" and he couldn't understand it. But on a Saturday afternoon you could guarantee that he'd be upstairs with his pipe in his mouth and he'd be watching the game on TV and no one was to disturb him! If somebody mentioned the game in the shop, he'd say, "I watched it but I didn't understand it; it's all changed!" Whether it was all an act, I don't know.'

In the early 1990s Gareth Davies authored a book with Peter Jones about Wrexham FC and met T.G. as part of his research. He recalled: 'When we wrote the Racecourse Robins book, Peter and I went to see Tommy at his shop in order to check what we'd written. He wasn't really welcoming – we got the impression that all was not well at home. I was amazed that he was more concerned with Marathon chocolate bars being renamed Snickers than talking about his footballing times. He looked at what we had written and said, "Fair enough." As we were leaving he said, "Don't forget the Bangor and Pwllheli days."'

Bangor City supporter Eric Thomas recalls Tommy's indifference to the club's performances: 'I remember going to the shop when he'd been retired from football a while. I asked him, "Do you ever come and watch Bangor?", and he said, "No, not likely. It's not my game any more. They're a lot of softies." I was quite downhearted, really. I'd hoped that he'd watch Bangor City now and again.'

Although some found his hospitality wanting, T.G. could be wonderful, engaging company when the mood took him. Andy Smith spent an afternoon in 1997 with T.G. while researching a biography of Tommy Lawton. 'T.G. was definitely not grumpy or gruff. He was in a really affable mood and gave generously of his time,' he remembered.

In 1990, Porthmadog-raised Everton supporter Geraint Williams was studying at Bangor University when a Sunday morning amble led to him establishing a friendly relationship with T.G. 'I went for a stroll down towards Bangor Pier. Being a big Evertonian, I was wearing my Toffees cap. I saw a newspaper shop and walked in. The man inside saw my cap and started talking about Everton. He was very reserved at first, maybe shy. He mentioned that he had played for them but didn't say much. I got into the habit of going in on a Sunday, and once he knew you were a regular and trusted you, you'd be able to have a good conversation with him. We'd have small conversations about what he thought about current Everton players. He had a constant disapproval about the amount of money in the game and the players of today having too much. There would be something on the back page of the paper and he'd say, "Have you seen this? That's a stupid amount of money." Now and again, he did speak a few words of Welsh, depending on his mood, which was surprising with him coming from Connah's Quay, where English dominates. The newsagent's seemed pretty busy on Sundays – it always seemed to be him behind the counter but when you walked in the smell of Sunday lunch was always wafting from the kitchen. He came across as a kind gentleman, not the boasting type at all.'

T.G. was recognised for his immense contribution to Welsh Football by the FAW at a ceremony held in 1993 at a Bangor hotel. The lifetime achievement award was bestowed on him by Elfed Ellis, President of the Football Association of Wales. Ellis was an avowed Evertonian who had seen T.G. in his playing pomp. Summing up his speech, Ellis enquired of the assembled audience, 'Who knows what T.G. stands for?' He went on to answer his own question, which visibly met with T.G.'s approval: 'Too Good for centre-forwards'.

Although often reticent and wary with those he did not know well, T.G. could be wonderful, engaging company when the mood took him. Andy Smith spent an afternoon with T.G. while researching a biography of Tommy Lawton. 'T.G. was definitely not grumpy or gruff. He was in a really affable mood and gave generously of his time.' Smith was not the only sportswriter or football enthusiast seeking out T.G. in person or via post in the 1990s. Many reporters were beguiled by T.G.'s presence and recall, which was virtually undimmed despite the passing of time. In 1997 he could not hide his amazement at the level of attention he continued to receive: 'I still get sent autograph books and letters from people – it is unbelievable that at this time of my life they still write to me. And that makes me wonder that we must have been more entertaining than the present-day players. I have difficulty remembering some of the players from last season!'[(AS)] Reporters were beguiled by T.G.'s presence and knowledge, which was virtually undimmed despite the passing of time.

One Evertonian who beat a path, as man and boy, to the door of the most famous newsagent in North Wales was Phil Parker. He recalls his encounters with him: 'As a young boy in the late 1960s, I was taken by my father to meet the great man at his shop near the pier in Bangor. I was maybe nine or ten. I obviously did not know who he was, but I could tell by my father's attitude in his presence that he was someone special to him. I remember that he had a huge shock of hair. In the summer of 1995, I took my own boys to Bangor. We headed for the same shop, and there he was, still with the hair! The boys didn't know who he was, but this time I was awestruck. I asked him if he was who I thought, and he said, "Well, who the bloody hell do you think I am?" – Marvellous!'

Sadly, around this time T.G.'s opinion of Everton had reached a nadir. With much of the household income spent on holidays in warmer climes, T.G. had not saved significant funds for his later years. One friend recalls, 'When I bumped into him he'd say: "As soon as I get a thousand pounds in the bank I can go on holiday."' Everton had recently been purchased by the Wirral businessman Peter Johnson, in the wake of the death of majority shareholder Sir John Moores. T.G. either gifted or sold most of his Everton-related possessions to the club. It was a decision he regretted, going to his grave believing – rightly or wrongly – that the club had misled him as to the value of the items.

In this climate of distrust, football historian David France approached T.G. in 1999 with a view to bringing him back into the Everton family. It proved to be a tall task. Before meeting T.G. he sought the counsel of former teammate Gordon Watson. Watson encouraged Dr France to meet T.G., but warned him of his grievances. These included the premature break-up of the 1939 title-winning team, the war, the club's refusal to let him leave in the late 1940s, and a feeling of under-appreciation from the club – particularly for his efforts during the war. Dr France recalls the time they spent together: 'I spent afternoons with T.G. and his wife Joyce in Bangor in an attempt to coax him to the second of Gwladys Street's Hall of Fame dinners, and then, hopefully, to Goodison. I would like to claim that he warmed to me but, in truth, the 81-year-old treated me with a level of suspicion usually reserved for the VAT man. Until my first meeting with T.G., I had assumed that old footballers were sweet-natured. I think it is fair to say that he was a 'bitter Blue'. He liked the adulation and had a soft spot for a few of his old teammates, but didn't have a good word to say about Everton Football Club and refused to participate in any Everton function.

'Eventually, he invited me for a spin in his car. With his mind concentrating on the narrow and winding streets of Bangor, I asked about his famous initials. "Thomas Gwynfor," he lied. At the tearoom at the end of the pier, Thomas George Jones wanted to chat about one thing and one thing only – his aborted move to Italy in 1948. I listened to his words. It had been fifty years ago but he had not forgiven those involved. He was not embarrassed to enlighten me that he earned more money and enjoyed more respect from the "Welsh tongues" in Pwllheli. Later that afternoon, I confessed that he was the most cantankerous old Blue I had encountered. In response, he claimed to be flattered by my choice of adjective!'

After much cajoling, Dr France was ultimately successful in persuading T.G. to attend the Gwladys Street's Hall of Fame dinner, held at Liverpool's Adelphi Hotel in 2000: 'After months of massaging his ego, which involved assuring him that he would have ranked above John Charles as Britain's finest footballing export, I agreed to his demands for attending the second event. They included a door-to-door taxi and an appearance fee. T.G., who addressed himself regularly in the third person, was well received by the fans. Shortly after he had taken his seat at the top table, I handed over a cheque for £1,000. The next time I glanced in his direction, I noticed that he hadn't even tasted his soup before vanishing back to North Wales.'

Before his premature bolt back across the border, T.G. had been reunited with Gordon Watson. His old teammate would pass away just weeks later. When Stan Bentham died in 2002, it left T.G. as the last survivor of Everton's 1939 Championship-winning team.

T.G. passed on the opportunity to grace Goodison Park one last time when, in January 2000, Everton welcomed its Millennium Giants for each decade onto the pitch at half-time. As the club's chosen 'Giant of the 1940s', this would have been a fitting final opportunity for T.G. to stand alongside Howard Kendall, Brian Labone, Alex Young and Dave Hickson in the centre-circle and receive the acclaim of those who had seen or heard of his deeds in the royal blue shirt. Instead, his daughter collected the framed certificate from Goodison Park several weeks later. Back home T.G. was persuaded by his daughter to pose for a snapshot with it in his living room. In contrast, later that month, the city of Bangor was able to express its appreciation of T.G.'s contribution to its sporting life when he was inducted as an honorary freeman of the city at a ceremony held at Penrhyn Hall. Bangor councillor and lifelong Evertonian Eddie Dogan would later comment: 'I bestowed the freeman honour on Tommy; it was one of my proudest moments.' After receiving the award T.G. strolled down to the kiosk operated on Bangor Pier by Glenis Pearce. T.G. had remained on cordial terms with her late father, Emrys Edwards, after leaving Bangor City – Edwards often called in at his shop for matches and a chat. A clearly emotional T.G. told her, 'If it wasn't for Emrys I wouldn't have achieved what I did and I wouldn't be here talking to you today.'

The newsagent's shop closed its doors for the last time in the mid-1990s – a sad day for the family. T.G. and Joyce would continue to live in the same property on Garth Road, receiving a local authority grant to help cover the costs of installing central heating and converting the tiny shop area into a living room.

As late in life as the autumn of 2002, T.G. was still taking regular exercise. He told Keith Evans: 'I swim every morning at the nearby pool, doing five or six lengths. I try to get in there early, before the students.'[DP] Ironically, in light of him having once been a regular swimmer in the sea, T.G. would frequently grumble that the pool temperature was too cold. Perhaps seeking more heat, he visited a Llandudno sauna on a weekly basis.

Although T.G. retained an impressive physical robustness in his final years, family and friends started to notice changes in his personality. This marked the onset of vascular dementia, resulting from a restricted blood supply to the brain. After T.G. died, medical staff indicated to his daughters that the most likely cause of the ailment had been nearly three decades spent heading heavy leather footballs.

The dementia would eventually manifest itself in the form of violent episodes. For everyone's wellbeing, T.G. was taken into nursing-home care in Penmaenmawr, and subsequently in Beaumaris, on his beloved Anglesey. He would spend most of the final months of his eighty-six years at a nursing home in Deganwy, near Llandudno. Loyal friends such as Iorys Griffiths and Ifor Roberts continued to visit him right until the end. One of Ifor Roberts' last, poignant, memories of T.G. is of seeing Iorys Griffiths helping his frail friend to light and hold a pipe. Glenis Pearce recalls: 'Iorys and his wife, Helen, were fantastic. They supported Tommy when he was ill with dementia and needed help. Tommy himself showed great courage in dealing with the illness that he had.'

A broken hip, sustained in a fall, saw T.G. hospitalised at Ysbyty Gwynedd in

Bangor. Here, he passed away on 3 January 2004 as a consequence of a rupture of the aorta – the large blood vessel leading from the heart. Joyce had lost her long battle with cancer the previous September.

Tributes flooded in from around the UK, especially from Merseyside and North Wales. The Professional Footballers' Association and the Everton Former Players' Foundation had given some support to T.G. in the sunset of his life; he had not been slow in coming forward to ask for financial help. Although feeling animosity towards many things related to Everton, T.G. was genuinely appreciative of the work done by the recently formed Foundation – particularly the assistance provided to former teammates less fortunate than himself. 'Goodison has been waiting fifty years for such a breath of fresh air,' he had told David France, the founder of the registered charity. Now, upon his passing, the Former Players' Foundation stepped in to cover all the costs of the funeral arrangements.

The service took place at Bangor Crematorium on 8 January, with T.G.'s ashes being scattered in the Garden of Remembrance. Norah Mercer, Tommy 'T.E.' Jones and Tony McNamara were among those with Everton connections who paid their respects. Bangor City FC was well represented, and it was Ken Birch, the club captain in those halcyon early years of the 1960s, who gave the eulogy. In it, he recalled, with tongue only partially in cheek, that he only saw T.G. worried once – when Napoli had wanted to exchange shirts with Bangor City's players after the match. T.G.'s reaction had been to rush onto the pitch exclaiming: 'Stop – we only have one set!'

The previous evening, T.G.'s passing had been marked at the stadium he had graced for fourteen years when Everton took on Arsenal. Ian Doyle of the Daily Post reported: 'A minute's silence following the death of Goodison legend T.G. Jones was observed as impeccably as the centre-half was said to have played his football for the Blues.'

The Farrar Road faithful showed their appreciation and respect in the same fashion three days later prior to a match against TNS. T.G.'s contribution to football has subsequently been commemorated by plaques at Connah's Quay Civic Hall and at Goodison Park. On the main stand wall at Goodison Park, T.G.'s signature adorns an 'Everton Giant' plaque displayed alongside those honouring the likes of Tommy Lawton, Joe Mercer, Ted Sagar and Bill 'Dixie' Dean. In 2017, as the 100th anniversary of his birth approached, Tommy was the inaugural inductee into Connah's Quay Nomads' Hall of Fame. A fitting tribute to the club's founding father.

So what is T.G.'s legacy? His cultured, daring, playing style at centre-half was anathema in a period when British football was becoming increasingly regimented and conservative in style. In the decades which followed, few centre-backs broke free of their defensive shackles as he once had. Colin Todd in the 1970s and Alan Hansen in the 80s demonstrated some of T.G.'s calmness on the ball and positional awareness, but according to first-hand witnesses of both it was Franz Beckenbauer's style that bore a closer resemblance to T.G.'s.

When asked, in 1997, how he might have adapted to modern football, T.G. himself was surprisingly unsure: 'I'd love to be playing today but I have no idea where I'd fit in. My style was completely different to anything you see today.'(AS) In the years since his passing, the game has evolved further. T.G. would no doubt excel in any present-day elite European team at centre-back, or as a deep-lying central midfielder with the ability to shield his back-line, dominate in the air and stride forward purposefully with the ball.

On his home turf, his talents have not been forgotten, and older Evertonians still speak in awe of T.G.'s mastery. In Bangor, 'Spirit of '62' was daubed onto the St Paul's End wall of Farrar Road, until its demolition, serving as a reminder of those epic encounters in Europe and the Welsh Cup. In 2009, Daily Post readers voted T.G. second only to Ian Rush as the greatest footballer to hail from North Wales. This outcome was in spite of T.G. not having kicked a ball in fifty years. It seems remiss, therefore, that T.G. has not, to date, been inducted into the English Football Hall of Fame, where he would join Everton teammates Tommy Lawton and Joe Mercer, as well as fellow-countrymen Billy Meredith, John Charles, Ivor Allchurch, Cliff Jones, Ian Rush, Mark Hughes and Neville Southall.

As a man, T.G. was, like all of us, merely human and flawed, but to those who saw him play on the football stage, he was godlike. Orig Williams paid a fitting and touching tribute in the Daily Post to the friend he idolised until the end:

> *After his death he was referred to by the press as 'The Prince of Centre-Halves'. But he was known during his career as 'The Prince of Wales'. God bless 'The Prince of Wales'.*

MEMORIES OF T.G.
Football Colleagues' Memories

William Ralph 'Dixie' Dean (Everton)

'He was the best centre-half in the game, though he seemed to be asleep half the time. The point was, though, that he even when he was asleep he played better than anybody else on the field.'

(When asked, in 1977, who was the greatest footballer he ever saw)

'He would have to be an Evertonian: T.G. Jones, the Welsh international centre-half. The best all-round player I've ever seen. He had everything – no coach could ever teach him anything. He was neater than John Charles. John looked awkward whereas Tommy would get out of a ruck by just opening his legs, letting the ball run wide and all this sort of thing – just letting it run through...'

Tommy Lawton (Everton)

'T.G. had the great ability to stroke the ball and he had the best right foot in the business. He was never satisfied with his performance and always drove the sides on. He was calm in a crisis and both delicate and sophisticated on the ground.'

Ted Sagar (Everton)

'In my opinion, the greatest centre-half I played with was T.G. Jones. What an artist he was. Cool and dominating, he had a habit of casually back-heading centres to me. This was a feature of the understanding we had. Mind you, we did come unstuck once and then the ball whistled past me from six yards' range. But he was a supreme centre-half. To my mind, only John Charles proved T.G.'s equal.'

'Tommy Jones, the football artist in anybody's language and one who does – and gets away with – things nobody else would think of attempting.' (Quoted in 1949)

Joe Mercer (Everton)

'He was unique. A good footballer with a delicate touch and the best long-ball player for ages.'

Harry Catterick (Everton)

'T.G. Jones was a very cultured centre-half. He was one of those fellows who was so accomplished and had so much time with which to play. The only player I have seen who was comparable is Johnny Carey.'

Gordon Watson (Everton)

'If I was really pressed to nominate the greatest-ever Everton player I would have to go for T.G. Jones. Forget about Bobby Moore and John Charles, T.G. was the most polished British defender of all time. His aristocratic style and uncommon ability to stroke the ball around when under pressure seduced football purists. T.G. was super-confident. He even headed corner kicks back to Ted Sagar. I called him "Cryogenic Jones".'

Norman Greenhalgh (Everton)

'Tommy Jones was a class centre-half, who also had astonishing ability on the ball for a defender.'

Stan Bentham (Everton)

'The 1938/39 team which won the title, in my view, was the best team that Everton ever had. There were ten great players and me. Tommy Jones and Billy Cook were defenders with the skills of an inside-forward.'

Tommy Clinton (Everton)

'T.G. Jones oozed class. He would have reigned supreme in this day and age.'

Dave Hickson (Everton)

'The first time I saw Goodison's magnificent structure I was in awe. As if in a dream, Joe Mercer greeted me along with T.G. Jones, the great Welsh international centre-half. I was a nobody, a strapping teenaged hopeful... but they took the time to welcome me, make me feel at home, as if I were a contender. It is something I have never forgotten.'

Will Cuff (Everton director)

TOM JONES – MY IDEAL CENTRE HALF
26 FEBRUARY 1949,
THE LIVERPOOL FOOTBALL ECHO
A STYLE OF HIS OWN –
AND A GRAND COACH

I have no love for mere stopping tactics that have become the foundation of most modern football sides. Rather would I have on my side the 'Tom Jones' type. He has been tried as centre-forward and inside-forward....but he is the natural centre half-back by birth and upbringing. He has the height, the flair for sizing up the next move of a forward, eyes glued to the ball, and heading ability.

CAREFUL PLACING

I like even better than those factors, his side-footed delivery of the ball and his infinite care to place the ball to a fellow player – in that phase he has no superior today, although Carey of Manchester United runs him close. He plays nothing but the game, aims at the greatest arts of defence and forcing attacks. You cannot escape or miss a Tommy Jones. His figure is upstanding, his style is his own, he has no copyists and I imagine some officials seeing him dallying with the ball in the goalmouth must suffer agonies of heart trouble lest in these close-goal movements he loses the ball.

It is nothing to them that he has probably saved twenty goals by his hesitance to get the ball away, and their only fear is that he might be robbed of the ball before he has got it to his comrades. Fear and football oft go hand-in-hand.

In recent years, schools have had the privilege of Tom Jones as their coach…he can instil into them the futility of the fool's cry of 'Get rid of it' by showing them an easy way out by means of a pass to the wingman. There is hope for football of the future so long as we have men of the Jones stamp to make their football impress upon the boys of our schools.

H. Gibbs (Birmingham City) in November 1938

'Six-foot Tommy Jones has proved his worth at centre-half. He is a fine stopper and generally comes out best in his duel with the centre-forward. But he doesn't only stop the other team – he feeds his forwards in really brainy style and has initiated, to my own knowledge, some really dangerous attacking movements.

'More than once in an encounter with Everton I have found my position rapidly changed from an observer of our own forwards to an active participator as a result of the clever way in which Jones has initiated an attack and changed the whole balance of the game.'

Cyril Done (Liverpool FC)

'A gentleman off the field and a gentleman on the field. I think he was the only player I ever knew who would dribble the ball on his own six-yard line and come out with it still between his feet.'

Norah Mercer (wife of Joe Mercer)

'T.G. was known as "The Uncrowned Prince of Wales". He used to have a great saying. If a player was playing badly, he used to say: "Is his wife pregnant?"'

Brian Labone (Everton)

'A member of the Goodison School of Science class of 1939, the Wales centre-half excelled at using his ball skills to play his way out of danger.'

Tommy Welsh (Blaenau Ffestiniog FC and Holyhead Town FC):

'What a player, what a gentleman. In 1953 I was posted to Kinmel Army Camp and had been there only three to four weeks when I signed for Blaenau Ffestiniog. My second game for them was against T.G., the player-manager of Pwllheli FC. I played against him in a lot of games and never once did he commit a foul against me. While playing for Holyhead it was always tough against him and his great squad of players. Although I scored a few goals as a centre-forward against him, he never played dirty. His skill won him the ball and we always shook hands. He was a true gentleman of sport.'

Alun Hughes (Pwllheli FC)

'I used to play in the Welsh League for Penmaenmawr, I was in the quarrying business and spent one season with T.G. before I had to move to South Wales. He approached me asking if I'd go to Pwllheli, which was a bit of a step up for me. 'Although he was coming to the end of his playing career, Tommy was a class apart in a really good team. He was a champion, on and off the field. I cherish the memories of playing with such a footballing great.

'North Wales lacked any education on playing – you just went out there and kicked the ball. Tommy was very good – he gave us the knowledge – he'd pull your back to the penalty-area line and tell you not to let the attacker any further in. Tommy would tell you to use a bit of common sense in passing the ball. He'd say: "Look, from the left-hand side put it over to the right-winger, if you can, with a through ball." You started picking things up yourself with the education you were getting. Tommy would tell you – he'd encourage you and tell you when you were not fit or had not been playing well.

'I remember that in one game we were playing St Helens in a preliminary round of the FA Cup. It was very wet and we were losing 1–0. He did not want to get knocked out as you could earn more money in the next round. With ten minutes to go he was shouting like hell, then our centre-forward equalised and we nearly won the match. After it had finished he got us into the dressing room and said: "Shut that bloody door." With the two directors there he said, "This crowd is not bloody fit." He told about four of them to get down to Bootle to train and told me to get out on Penmaenmawr Sands. He worked through the whole team actually and we beat St Helens in the return match!

Roy Matthews (Bangor City)

'What Tommy Jones achieved at Bangor with a bunch of part-timers was quite outstanding. It is testimony to his motivational skills and presence that he only had the team together for approximately one hour in which to get his message across before every home game. He had that self-assured confidence. Tommy looked the part and was charismatic in the true sense of the word – and a handsome bugger as well! My initial impressions stayed with me throughout all the years that I played for him. A lot of things that he promised when I joined proved to be right – I had five glorious years at Bangor.

'The one, and only, time I attended an actual pre-season training session at Bangor was in 1963 when I happened to be in Porthmadog on holiday and Tom invited me over to take part. We had a five-a-side game over the full pitch and Tommy, who was in his forties, played. What was remarkable was that he didn't run but was hitting thirty/forty-yard passes with astonishing accuracy. The only other person I've seen who was that good was Glenn Hoddle.'

Jim Conde (Bangor City)

'He was very, very confident and sure of himself, but not in a nasty way. He always had a good opinion. He was the top man in that Bangor area and he knew it. I can still see him now with this mop of black curly hair. He knew his pull; he had an aura about him which transposed to all of us. He just had something about him that made you want to play for him.'

Supporters' Memories

Hal Leonard

'My grandfather took me to Goodison for the first time – he worshipped T.G. I was around ten to twelve years old when he was playing. I cried when Joe Mercer (a wonderful player, and a lovely man, but hard on the pitch) and Tommy Lawton left and was so disappointed if T.G. was not picked.

'I have never seen a better centre-half than T.G. Jones, and that includes John Charles. He had a wonderful way of kicking the ball – he could punt it. T.G. was the personification of coolness, the crowd wanted him to get rid of the ball but I didn't understand why. They were frightened that he might lose the ball but he never did. He was never riled – you had to be a bit naughty to play in the 1940s and 50s but he didn't need to be – he was above them. They were privileged to be on the same pitch as him. It's a shame that he never got the recognition he deserves.'

Neville Powell

'The very first game I saw Everton play was during the war when the Football League had been disbanded and there were local leagues. Everton played against Wrexham at the Racecourse Ground and T.G. was playing along with Tommy Lawton and they were way ahead of anybody I've seen. T.G. was very unusual; it was an era of stopper centre-halves as they had been pulled back to become a third back. But he managed to do both jobs. What was astonishing about him was that instead of hoofing the ball he dribbled the ball out of his own penalty area to take it upfield. He had tremendous ball control to carry it out and start a counterattack. The only player who could compare with T.G. was Franz Beckenbauer – he was very similar in that he could start an attack and was not just content to get rid.'

Jimmy Erskine

'To me, T.G. Jones was the finest footballer that I've ever seen. He was a big Welsh lad with black curly hair and he moved, more or less, in a circle. A beautiful player. I've never seen his equal yet.'

Dave Abrahams

'I saw T.G. Jones through the eyes of a seven-and eight-year-old boy in the late 1940s. I used to just marvel at his coolness and ability. He would just stroll through a game, seeing everything seconds before anyone else, he always seemed to stay on his feet and came off the pitch without a mark on his shorts, even on the muddiest pitches. An immaculate performer. Something happened at the club because Cliff Britton, the manager, dropped him and he was out of the team for a long period. It was most definitely Everton's loss when he left the club.'

David Peate

'People compare T.G. to Franz Beckenbauer but T.G. was more than just a cultured back-stop. He was much more like the (later) Jim Baxter. T.G. controlled the midfield with unerring accuracy. Everton's fluent football started with him as he splayed accurate passes all over the field. He was an advocate of playing forward, not sideways or backwards. He was elegant, cool, clean and nonchalant. I cannot remember seeing him ever being put in the referee's little book. He was revered by the Everton faithful.

'T.G. was overlooked for first-team appearances on numerous occasions. Falder and Humphreys often preceded him in the pecking order. Both were far inferior players. I remember the report in the Liverpool Echo which said something like, "Jack Humphreys was not a Tommy Jones" but that he was "adequate". I recall my family's reaction to that crass statement. We didn't want "adequate", we wanted the best and that was T.G. It was risible.'

Jim King

'He was absolutely brilliant, cool under pressure, good in the air and brilliant on the ground. What always stands out in my opinion of T.G., if he took a free kick, say from the edge of his own box, he'd just stroll up, no effort at all, perfectly positioned, correct kicking and all that, and the ball would zoom into the other penalty area. The man was absolute perfection.'

Eddie Dogan

'When I was a boy growing up in Bangor, myself and a few other Everton fans would save up to go to Goodison once a season and it would be a big day out for us. When we got there our idol was Tommy Jones; he was the idol of all the Everton fans because he was a terrific player.

'I would put him in a category above Bobby Moore because he was so talented with both feet and so clever. If he was around today no one could afford him, he was that good, one of the greatest players I ever saw.'

Ray Terry

'T.G. was one of my all-time heroes. People often ask me who the greatest players I have seen during my many years of watching football are. My five greats are John Charles, Duncan Edwards, Tom Finney, T.G. Jones and Billy Liddell, and I would not like to separate them. Edwards and Liddell were rugged but very fair, John Charles could be rugged and a bit classical, but Finney and T.G. were sheer classical players and a joy to watch. T.G. could hit the ball like a mule and could also bend its flight long before the modern ball came into use. He was a superb tackler and a great reader of a game. At centre-half, when he rose for a header and he could not see anybody to head it to, he would back-head it to the goalkeeper. When Ted Sagar was in goal they often had "words". He was a complete footballer, an immaculate passer and header of the ball, and I cannot remember him ever being cautioned. He really was a joy to watch. I suppose the nearest player to T.G.'s style of play was probably Alan Hansen of Liverpool, but Hansen was not as good.'

Peter Rooney

'T.G. played the game like it was in slow motion, it looked effortless. He was a powerful man but he moved like a dancer. He never rushed when on the ball, he was one of the finest passers of the ball, was graceful with and without the ball at his feet. He never jumped into a tackle but just strolled in and took the ball from the opposition, absolute class.

He wasn't a dirty player, and though he was a big man he never used his weight or size to gain any advantage against the opponent, and he never grabbed anyone, unlike Hansen! I never saw him intentionally cheat, as far as I can remember.

If he was playing today he would be worth hundreds of millions. It was absolutely marvellous to watch him play.'

John Hughes

'I remember in the early 1970s I was in Bangor with my son, who was seven or eight years of age at the time. We were walking down to the pier where T.G. had a small shop. The great man was on his way home after doing fifty-odd lengths at the swimming baths. I said to my son, "That man played for us," so he asked T.G. if he played football with Alan Ball. T.G. smiled, ruffled my son's hair, and said, "No, but I wish we had played at the same time." We had a little chat about our team. It was a pleasure to talk to the great man – he was a True Blue Legend.'

Jimmy Battle

'I have to say that Tommy was one of the best players I ever saw. Being an Everton supporter all my life, I saw a lot of him from when football started again after the Second World War until his retirement. These players cited him as the best player they had ever seen: Tommy Lawton, Stanley Matthews, Joe Mercer, Dixie Dean, Tom Finney. How's that for a reference? I have to mention another player I thought was a great: John Charles, who was another gentleman on and off the field. John played the game clean like Tommy, no rough stuff. But I still rate Jones as my number one. Never a show-off, tall and cool in all encounters, never got flustered or panicky, a two-footed player and a great header of the ball. The best free-kicker of a ball I ever saw from any range. He could land a ball on a dime. Opposition corner kicks were mostly taken care of by Tommy's headers. I can't remember ever seeing Tommy knock anyone down in a tackle, and he never argued a referee's decision for or against him – he just got on with the game.

'I have enjoyed jogging my memory about this legend who never actually got the credit or notice he deserved in our world of soccer.'

Eric Owen

'I was living in Teulon Street, just off Walton Lane, when I started collecting Everton players' autographs in 1937, and can't remember the number of hours I stood outside the Players' Entrance on Goodison Road.

'I well remember all the players, having met them and got their autographs many, many times. These were: Ted Sagar, Billy Cook, Norman Greenhalgh, Cliff Britton, Charlie Gee, Jock Thomson, Albert Geldard, Joe Mercer, Torry Gillick, Stan Bentham, Alex Stevenson, Tommy Lawton and Dixie Dean. These were the players who never ever refused giving an autograph to a kid. Sometimes, they would look through your autograph book and tell you they had already signed but then they would sign again.

'If you looked closely, you would have seen two names missing: Wally Boyes and T.G. Jones. Very rarely Wally Boyes would relent and sign but I only knew one boy who had T.G.'s autograph. This was because Mr Ernest Green, Everton's chairman in the late 1930s, was a school teacher at Walton Lane School at the top of Fountains Road where I attended.

'Mr Green informed all the kids that he would get the autographs of the complete team for the best fourteen-year-old pupil who would be leaving school that year. Not me, I'm afraid – I was too young. Even though T.G. would never sign, he was still held in the highest esteem by the kids who just regarded him as a challenge. But I did have Boyes' autograph as one day he asked me to go on an errand for him to a Walton Lane shop, a newsagent's at the top of Spellow Lane. When I returned he signed my book. Sorry to say, I lost all my autographs when we were bombed out of Teulon Street on 18 November 1940.

'This story is a kid's perspective of a player, but I well remember, when I saw him play, how cool, calm and collected he was as he stood head and shoulders above the opposition centre-forward. You mustn't forget we won the First Division in 1939 and held the title for the following six years. Maybe the war had something to do with that, but it still sounds good!'

Barry G. Jones
'In March 1948 my Uncle Gwil received passes from T.G. to see Everton play Grimsby. He scored one of his rare goals as well as providing a pass for Billy Higgins' goal. Another time he got us passes for a match against Blackpool in 1949. We won 5–0 and T.G. provided a superb pass for one of Eddie Wainwright's four goals.

'T.G. was asked to present the school prizes in 1957 when I was at Friars Grammar in Bangor. He looked very tall and elegant in a grey Prince of Wales check suit. He was always elegantly dressed in a camel overcoat or sometimes a trench coat. He could often be seen at the Premier, a tobacconist's near to the cinema. He smoked a pipe and, I believe, had a weakness for San Toy cigarillos.'

Bill Dudley

'Tommy was the man that started us off at Connah's Quay Juniors. He was involved a lot behind the scenes. He taught a lot of the youngsters to play good football. You would see him walking down to Shotton station to take the train to training at Everton. I considered him one of the finest centre-halves in the world at that time. A fantastic footballer: tall, and he knew how to head a ball. He was good at anything.

'Last year I got talking to some ladies from Liverpool and we got talking about Tommy. They said, "Oh, he was a film star, he was beautiful. We all fell for him."'

Ken Aston

'I went to a sportsman's dinner in Mostyn with Stan Mortensen and Duncan McKenzie as after-dinner speakers. My friend Chick Smallwood said to me: "I'm going to ask Stan Mortensen a question now and I know the answer before he tells me." So he stood up and said: "Mr Mortensen, who was the best centre-half you ever played against?" Mortensen replied, "T.G. Jones. I scored goals against him but he was the best centre-half." [And Chick said]: "There you go, I told you so!"'

Geoff Threlfall (Connah's Quay Juniors/Nomads)

'Tommy was a great man, well respected in these parts. He was "Mr Connah's Quay Nomads" and it would be nice to think something could be done in his memory. There are youngsters growing up who know nothing about Tommy and his achievements. That saddens me because he was such a distinguished man who took an interest in the wellbeing of the youth of Connah's Quay.'

Gwyn Jones (son of Dr Idris Jones, who helped bring T.G. to Pwllheli)

'When my father was terminally ill in 1971, there was a knock on the door, and when I opened it there was T.G. Jones, who had kindly come, unannounced, all the way from Bangor to see him. I think they had a nice conversation for the best part of an hour. I held Tommy in the highest regard because of that. I have memories of him playing for Pwllheli. In one particular match he took a free kick from outside the penalty area and the next thing I just saw it in the back of the net. He hit it so hard that it was like a rocket.

'I remember Tommy speaking once and he was a very authoritative man as far as football was concerned. I had the impression that what Tommy said, you did. On the football field he was the one directing the others, telling them, "You go this way – you go that way."'

Grahame Boulter (son of Les Boulter, T.G.'s Wales teammate and predecessor at Pwllheli FC)
'I've got fond memories of Tommy Jones. My dad ran two newsagent-tobacconist's in the town. Tommy and my dad were close friends and Tommy used to come to our house quite often. I used to call him "Uncle Tom". He and my father were on very equal terms, so I was not in awe that much in football terms. When he walked in he did have a certain presence about him. For me, as a young person, he seemed quite a smooth devil, with wavy hair, and an urbane type of chap.'

Ifor Roberts (Pwllheli FC and Bangor City)
'You have never seen a more vain man in all your life but he could also show great kindness. T.G. was a great, great centre-half – there are no two ways about it. The delightful Brian Labone said to me: "Do you know what Ifor? To the old fellas I'll always be number two to T.G. Jones." I was so impressed at Brian – an England centre-half – saying that. That's how well T.G. Jones was thought of.'

Dafydd Islwyn
'They talk about Gareth Bale now but Wales had a world-class star in the late 1940s with Tommy Jones. I saw him play for Pwllheli and especially when he was at Bangor. It was amazing to watch him as, even at that age and nearing the end of his career, he was an excellent player. It was a pleasure watching how he could read the game and put himself in the right position. He was so cool under pressure. One of his headers would get the ball rolling from the Bangor penalty area down the field.'

Elfed Ellis (President of the Football Association of Wales in 1993)
'What does the T.G. in T.G. Jones stand for? "Too Good for centre-forwards".'

T.G.'S PLAYING RECORD

WREXHAM

	LEAGUE		CUP	
	Appearances	Goals	Appearances	Goals
1935/36	6	0	0*	0
1941/42	5#	0	0	0
1942/43	2#	0	0	0
Total	13	0	0	0

Notes

* T.G. made 1 Welsh Cup and 1 Football League Northern Sections Cup appearance in 1935/56

Appearances in 1941/42 and 1942/43 seasons were as a wartime guest

EVERTON

	LEAGUE		FA CUP		WAR LEAGUE		WAR CUP		TOTAL	
	Apps	Goals	Apps	Goals	Apps	Goals	Apps	Goals	Apps	Goals
1936/37	1	0	0	0					1	0
1937/38	28	0	2	0					30	0
1938/39	39	0	5	0					44	0
1939/40	3[1]	3	0	0	16	3	4	2	23	5
1940/41*					27	1	6	1	33	2
1941/42*					23	6[2]	12	6	23	7
1942/43*					8	0	2	0	8	0
1943/44*					33	5	11	1	33	5
1944/45*					12	8	6	3	12	8
1945/46*			0	0	10	4			10	4
1946/47	22	3	1	1					23	4
1947/48	24	1	0	0					24	1
1948/49	37	0	2	0					39	0
1949/50	14	0	0	0					14	0

Notes

* All of the Football League War Cup games in these seasons also counted towards the relevant War Football League Championship. Games played and goals scored in these 'dual matches' have only been included once in the overall total.

[1] The 1939/40 Football League was abandoned after 3 games.

[2] T.G. Jones scored an extra-time goal in a League Championship/League War Cup 'dual' match at Preston in April 1942. The score after 90 minutes was counted as the result of the League match, so the extra-time goal is included in these statistics as only a War Cup goal.

SWANSEA TOWN (WARTIME GUEST)

	LEAGUE		CUP	
	Appearances	Goals	Appearances	Goals
1942/43	3	4	0	0
Total	**3**	**4**	**0**	**0**

TRANMERE ROVERS (WARTIME GUEST)

	LEAGUE		CUP	
	Appearances	Goals	Appearances	Goals
1940/41	1	0	0	0
Total	**1**	**0**	**0**	**0**

PWLLHELI

1950/51 to 1956/57 seasons (detailed statistics not available)

BANGOR CITY

1957/58 to 1958/59 seasons (detailed statistics not available)

INTERNATIONAL CAREER FOR WALES (PEACETIME)

DATE	VENUE		OPPONENTS	RESULT	
16 March 1938	Belfast	A	Ireland	L	0-1
22 October 1938	Cardiff	H	England	W	4-2
9 November 1938	Edinburgh	A	Scotland	L	2-3
15 March 1939	Wrexham	H	Ireland	W	3-1
19 October 1946	Wrexham	H	Scotland	W	3-1
13 November 1946	Manchester	A	England	L	0-3
18 October 1947	Cardiff	H	England	L	0-3
12 November 1947	Glasgow	A	Scotland	W	2-1
10 March 1948	Wrexham	H	Ireland	W	2-0
10 November 1948	Villa Park	A	England	L	0-1
9 March 1949	Belfast	A	Ireland	W	2-0
15 May 1949	Lisbon	A	Portugal	L	2-3
22 May 1949	Liege	A	Belgium	L	1-3
26 May 1949	Berne	A	Switzerland	L	0-4
15 October 1949	Cardiff	H	England	L	1-4
9 November 1949	Glasgow	A	Scotland	L	0-2
23 November 1949	Cardiff	H	Belgium	W	5-1

INTERNATIONAL CAREER FOR WALES (WARTIME)

Date	Venue		Opponents	Result	
11 November 1939	Cardiff	H	England	D	1-1
18 November 1939	Wrexham	H	England	L	2-3
7 June 1941	Cardiff	H	England	L	2-3
25 October 1941	Birmingham	A	England	L	1-2
24 October 1942	Molineux, Wolverhampton	A	England	W	2-1
27 February 1943	Wembley	A	England	L	3-5
8 May 1943	Ninian Park, Cardiff	H	England	D	1-1
25 September 1943	Wembley	A	England	L	3-8
4 May 1946	Ninian Park, Cardiff	H	Ireland	L	0-1

ACKNOWLEDGEMENTS

In the course of researching and writing this book over two years, I have become indebted to many people for their assistance and encouragement.

First of all, sincere thanks go to my family. Paula, Sian and Ceri have exhibited their customary understanding and patience during the gestation period. My sister, Louise, was her customary, supportive self, prior to her passing.

Dafydd Islwyn, Bangor City supporter and an expert on North Wales football, encouraged me to tell T.G.'s story. Throughout the research process, he has provided newspaper material, performed translation duties and introduced me to numerous acquaintances of T.G..

T.G.'s daughter, Jane Jones, has been very generous with her time and given me access to images and documents. Other family members kindly shared their recollections, documents and photographs with me. These were Ceris Jones, Pam Roberts, Mark Thomas, Ian Jones, Chris Kozlowski, Raynor Pope and George Hawkes. Sadly, George passed away before this book was completed.

Special thanks go to John Rowlands, Rogan Taylor, Andrew Ward, John Williams, Andy Smith and David McVay for facilitating access to recordings and transcripts of interviews they conducted with T.G.

John Roberts, David France, Daniel Leeman, Jack Gordon-Brown, James Corbett and Ian Allen have proof-read or copy-edited the manuscript at various stages of its development.

Elis Jones, Ifor Roberts, John Cowell, Bernie Smith, Gareth Davies, Ioan Roberts, Keith Evans, Gwyn Jenkins (who unearthed several nuggets for me at the National Library of Wales) and Dafydd Whiteside Thomas were particularly helpful in my quest to learn about T.G.'s post-Everton days.

I consider myself privileged to be a member of EFC Heritage Society, an organisation dedicated to researching and chronicling the rich history of Everton Football Club. As always, my fellow members have come to my aid during the course of my research. Billy Smith, creator and curator of the wonderful Blue Correspondent website, has saved me from many hours of trawling microfilm archives for newspaper articles. Steve Johnson's book, Everton – The Official Complete Record, has consistently proved to be a godsend. George Orr, Paul Wharton, David Prentice, James Corbett, Ken Rogers and Neville Powell have all provided welcome assistance. Thomas Regan (Milkyone Creative) designed a striking cover which benefited from the incorporation of Mark Mordecai's illustration of Goodison Park. The Heritage Society's Founder, David France, not only provided a foreword but also shared with me recollections of his encounters with T.G. Kevin Ratcliffe generously provided a foreword about his predecessor for Everton and Wales, for which I am indebted to him.

I am also grateful to the following for their contributions to this project: Jack Murray, John Ogwen, Tommy Welsh, Alison Denton, Idris and Iris Evans, Eifion and Lena Jones, Steven Jones, Mark Currie, Gwyn Jones, Gwilym Owen, Gerry Humphreys, Jimmy Harris, Tom Cowell, Catherine Smith, Mary Morris Jones Bernad, Jane Bernad, Ernest Williams, Andrew Thomas, Jim Conde, Tony Broadhead, Melvyn Griffiths, Tom Gardner (1923–2016), Tony Ensor, Richard Parry, Ken Aston, Lyndon Lloyd (Toffeeweb), Nik Mesney (gap Connah's Quay), Darren Griffiths (Everton FC), Paul Davies, John Coppack, Neville Williams, Hal Leonard, Gerry Humphreys, John Britton, Joyce Catterick, Bill Dudley, Jimmy Battle, Andy Smith, Grahame Boulter, Geraint Williams, Dave Hughes, Dave Jones, Matt Johnson (Bangor City Supporters' Association), Eric Thomas,

Tommy Banks, John Hardy, Megan Corcoran (Storiel), Glynne Roberts, Reg Hunter, Gareth Hughes, Don Hardisty, Ian and Jenny Birch, Eurwyn Williams, Emyr ab Iorwerth, Emyr Evans, Ifan Howard Jones, Roy Matthews, Graham Griffiths, David Wright, Alun Hughes, David Peate, Barry G. Jones, Ian Jones, Phil Parker, Harold Matthews, Ray Terry, David Pearce, Terry Williams, Nathan and Peter Rooney and Glenis Pearce.

Local studies, archive and museum staff in Liverpool, Hawarden, Wrexham, Caernarfon and the National Library of Wales, were all helpful during the course of my research.

Amanda Lewis of repairmypicture.co.uk kindly restored some of the photographs reproduced in this book.

Finally, I thank the deCoubertin Books team for their support and expertise in bringing my project to publication.

If I have inadvertently omitted anyone from this list, please accept my apologies and thanks.

SOURCE MATERIAL

NEWSPAPERS AND PERIODICALS

Liverpool Daily Post
Liverpool Echo and Football Echo
Liverpool Evening Express
Daily Post (North Wales edition)
Picture Post
Caernarfon and Denbigh Herald
The North Wales Chronicle
Western Mail
The Leader (Wrexham and Chester editions)
The Times
The People
Daily Mirror
Daily Express
Daily Mail

Reynolds News
Charles Buchan's Football Monthly
Topical Times
Blue Blood magazine – George Orr
Everton FC programmes

ONLINE SOURCES

Blue Correspondent website by Billy Smith (www.bluecorrespondent.co.nr)
Everton board meeting minutes (www.evertoncollection.org.uk)
Welsh Football Data Archive (www.wfda.co.uk)
Steve Johnson's Everton Results website (www.evertonresults.com)
Bangor City independent website (www.the-citizens-choice.co.uk)

FILM, VIDEO AND RADIO

YouTube and British Pathé footage of Bangor City vs Napoli 1962
HTV
S4C – Cadw Cwmni gyda John Hardy (with Elis Jones)
Ffarwel Farrar Road (BBC Radio Cymru)

BOOKS

Three Sides of the Mersey – Rogan Taylor and Andrew Ward with John Williams (Robson Books, 1993)
Everton in the 1940s – 'The Lost Decade' – George Orr (Blue Blood Productions, 2013)
Everton: The Official Complete Record – Steve Johnson (deCoubertin Books, 2016)
Goodison Glory – Ken Rodgers (Breedon Books, 2000)
The Everton Encyclopedia – James Corbett (deCoubertin Books, 2012)
Everton: The School of Science – James Corbett (deCoubertin Books, 2010)
Gwladys Street's Blue Book – David France & David Prentice (Skript Publishing, 2002)
Gwlady's Street's Hall of Fame – David France (Skript Publising, 1999)
Everton: The Official Centenary History – John Roberts (Mayflower, 1978)

The Pride of North Wales Football – Mark Currie and Gareth Bicknell (Sport Media, 2009)

Who's Who of Welsh International Soccer Players – Gareth M. Davies and Ian Garland (Bridge Books, 1991)

The Complete Centre Forward: The Authorised Biography of Tommy Lawton – Dave McVay and Andy Smith (SportsBooks Ltd, 2003)

Get In There! – Tommy Lawton, My Friend, My Father – Barrie Williams & Tom Lawton Jr. (Vision Sports, 2010)

Football Is My Business – Tommy Lawton (Sporting Handbooks, 1948)

Soccer at War, 1939–45 – Jack Rollin (Headline, 2005)

The Cannonball Kid – Dave Hickson with James Corbett (deCoubertin Books, 2014)

Harry Catterick, The Untold Story of a Football Great – Rob Sawyer (de Coubertin Books, 2014)

Joe Mercer OBE: Football with a Smile – Gary James (James Ward, 2010)

Dixie Dean: The Inside Story of a Football Icon – John Keith (Robson Books, 2001)

Albert Geldard: The Life and Times of a Professional Footballer – Albert Geldard with John K. Rowlands (Countryside, 1989)

Everton Football Club: 1878–1946 – John K. Rowlands (The History Press, 2001)

Juniors to Nomads (Connah's Quay Nomads, 1953)

Connah's Quay and Shotton's Footballing History: 1918 to 1939 – Vic Williams (WD Books, 2005)

Farewell Farrar Road – Glynne Roberts (Bangor City Supporters' Association, 2012)

PelDroedwyr Sir Y Fflint – Steven Jones (Gwasg Carreg Gwalch, 2005)

El Bandito: The Story of Orig Williams – Orig Williams and Martyn Williams (Y Lolfa, 2010)

Ah'm Tellin' Thee: Tommy Banks: Bolton Wanderers and England – Ian Seddon (Paragon Publishing, 2014)

INDEX